TES

3, 2, 1

Published by Melbourne Books
Level 9, 100 Collins Street,
Melbourne, VIC 3000
Australia
www.melbournebooks.com.au
info@melbournebooks.com.au

Title: Testing 3, 2, 1: What Australian Education Can
Learn From Finland
Author: Michael Lawrence
ISBN: 9781925556926

A catalogue record for this
book is available from the
National Library of Australia

TESTING 3, 2, 1

WHAT AUSTRALIAN EDUCATION CAN LEARN FROM FINLAND

MICHAEL LAWRENCE

M

MELBOURNE BOOKS

CONTENTS

INTRODUCTION

... the aims of education are to enable students to understand the world around them and the talents within them so that they can become fulfilled individuals and active, compassionate citizens.

— English educationalist Sir Ken Robinson

It was connections made with Finnish fans of Australian music that took me to Finland, where I was able to get a first-hand look at their education system. As a schoolteacher of some thirty years' experience teaching from grade prep to year 12, in both government and non-government schools, I figured it would be valuable professional development. After all, Finland has the reputation of being the best in the world when it comes to education, so maybe I could find just what all the fuss is about and even borrow a few secrets.

Discussions with teachers and teacher trainers in Finland led me to re-evaluate the education system I had been a part of for three decades. I knew that Australian teachers were leaving the profession in great numbers, and student results were going backwards ... but I assumed we were doing all we could to counter this and that the methods we had adopted were backed up by solid research and the latest ideology. Like most Australian teachers, I had accepted the introduction of a standardised curriculum, standardised testing and student 'achievement standards' for as best practice for students and teachers alike.

But my trust was misplaced.

Finnish teachers looked at me as if I were a child molester when I described the NAPLAN tests given to children as young as eight. With shocked expressions, they asked why Australian teachers allowed this to be done to such young children. They then suggested that (of course) the results of these tests should lead to increased funding and assistance for those students and schools that did not do well.

There was no reasonable answer to this. My investigation into what made the Finnish system so successful was quickly becoming an inquiry into why my own system was so unsuccessful.

The next few years would see more time in Finland, more time in schools there and more time interacting with Finnish educators at all levels. Dozens of education books were read. Dissertations on Finnish education and teacher training, in addition to countless formal and informal interviews with

Australian and Finnish teachers, followed. How had Australia found itself in this position? Why?

Is there any research or proven ideology behind it?

The same had to be done in respect of the Finnish system. What did the latest educational thinking say? What does the neuroscience tell us?

What about the multinational testing of 15-year-olds' academic performance—that goes by the acronym PISA (Program for International Student Assessment)—that was pitting the world's educational systems against each other?

How do teachers fare in these systems? The Australian media headlines blame teachers for declining results from the NAPLAN tests and suggest that up to half of them are leaving the profession within five years of graduating. Most importantly, what about the students? How do they fare under the two systems?

If NAPLAN scores are always in decline, then why are we persisting with them and other aspects of the standardised system? Even Singapore has abandoned the idea that every student should be able to do certain things at a particular age and all those in the same grade should be ranked against one another.

SCHOOL DAYS

My experience of school as a student rather than a teacher was typical, I suspect, for the era. Primary school was a mixture of government and Catholic schools as my family moved house three or four times, though never leaving Melbourne's western suburbs. Our first moves were due to my father changing jobs and we relocated again after he passed away. In those days the western suburbs of Sunshine, North Altona and Albion were on the fringes of the 'country', and open fields were just a short walk away on the other side of Kororoit Creek.

Despite this 'country' feel (I was nearly going to say 'pastoral', but that would have been overdoing it: to my knowledge there were no poems written about Kororoit Creek), Melbourne's west was very much like an old car in the city's backyard. It had seen better days, such as before the Massey Ferguson (previously Sunshine Harvester) tractor factory shut down, but no-one was really prepared to fix it up, and many doubted it was worth fixing.

Schools were unforgiving places in the late sixties and seventies. Our sixth-grade classroom at Our Lady's adjoined the principal's (a nun's) office, giving our class's lessons a soundtrack of leather straps hitting hands (I hope that was all they were hitting!); a none too subtle reminder of why it was best to toe the line. This particular school had not a blade of grass anywhere on the asphalt playground, most of which was taken up by an imposing church the size of a small football ground itself (or so it seemed to this ten-year-old) and the height of a ten-storey building, casting a shadow over the schoolyard until at least midday. The terrifying boom of Father Murphy's voice truly sounded like it was coming from the depths of the hell he auctioned to the lowest bidder.

Secondary school was a Catholic boys' college, St John's Braybrook. Entry exams made it easy to identify those not suited to academic study and we were all placed in six or seven streamed classes with close to forty boys in each. I'd managed to scrape into the second from the top of these (St Luke), although any sense of accomplishment was lost on me, perhaps as I felt I'd had no say in the matter.

An avid reader since mid primary school, I devoured Jules Verne among others and was starting to take an interest in the music press, music becoming something of an outlet for my inner world particularly since my father's death.

My grade prep teacher had made me write with my right hand instead of the left I instinctively grabbed the pencil with, meaning my handwriting was never particularly 'neat'. Much to the amusement of classmates, my year 8 teacher described it as 'like spiders climbing on the blackboard'.

Classes were conducted with strict formality. Some teachers still addressed students by their surnames, and students got into the habit of calling every teacher 'Sir' or 'Miss'.

One teacher, rumoured to have been of German descent (to us at the time this as good as said 'Gestapo', and he certainly had a big, booming voice and accent so no-one ever dared ask him if it was true) and a large, completely bald man, had a habit of grasping students on the neck with a firmness that drew tears from terrified thirteen-year-olds. I've never forgotten sitting in this class and turning around to note that every face I saw had tears on it. As a young boy, the eldest of three brothers just recovering from the death of their father, my experience of secondary school was not the relief from the pressures of home that I might have hoped for. While I was anything but a 'bad' child, like most teenagers I would occasionally forget a small element of my homework and find myself in the firing line of pedantic teachers.

There were no subject choices to be made, although the top two of the streamed classes did not participate in any of the practical, or 'trade', subjects as we referred to them. So I missed out on woodwork and metalwork. Discipline was strict. Students who did not have their towel to dry themselves in the showers after sport (many were shy about doing so in front of the sports teacher who stood at the shower entrance observing the entire process very, very closely) were required to run extra laps of the sports oval, ironically making a shower even more necessary. I distinctly remember thinking that if I ever became a teacher I would do all I could to put a stop to these archaic practices. This is the earliest recollection I have of ever actually considering education as a career path, though the significance of the idea stemming from a belief that it could be done better rather than from a positive influence is not lost on me.

As was common in Catholic schools of the time, many of the teachers were religious brothers, and I can recall the entire class staying back after not taking our RE (religious education) studies seriously enough. Copying biblical passages word for word put an end to this poor behaviour (seemingly), and a *Sunday* detention (I'll never forget riding my bike to school in full uniform on Sunday—seemed to have forgotten about the Sabbath there) ensured the class—yes, the whole class—showed more respect for the science teacher whose real name escapes me. He was known to all as 'Weed', probably taken from the *Flower Pot Men* children's show. An opportunity to push back at the system saw an equally brutal response: that class probably ended a teacher's career.

Rather than having any number of subject options (I don't think I selected a subject until year 11) our class streams seemed to set a student's future in slow-drying cement: you were more likely to drown than change streams.

The first teacher to really have a positive influence on me was a year 11 legal studies teacher, Mr Brewster (I think his first name was Wayne). He used to bring legal studies to life by telling complicated, often humorous stories to illustrate his points, and his black denim trousers and shirt differentiated him from the formal business outfits of the other teachers. On the examination (exams made up 100 percent of many subject grades for the Higher School Certificate, forerunner of the VCE), the defendants in the court included Jimmy Page and Robert Plant, who had stolen from a certain Robert Dylan. Seeing as myself and my best mate had been removed from legal studies for a week for talking music constantly (Dean had argued that Kiss were better than Led Zeppelin, a greater crime than any mentioned by Mr Brewster all year) when we should have been concentrating on the class, this was a very deliberate move on the teacher's part to get our attention and let us know that he was aware of our outside interests.

Placing our music idols in the exam paper (another villain he included was a certain Warren Bruiser, who had viciously assaulted one Jean Simmons, a lady of the night) ensured our eternal respect and framed legal studies in a manner that a couple of teenagers more interested in the sounds coming from the radio could relate to. This was the first time I can recall a teacher trying to bring together the world that I lived in and the world I inhabited at school.

The humour of Brewster and a senior English teacher (a Miss or Mrs Doolan) who encouraged me to write some music reviews for the school newspaper (I believe one of Cold Chisel's *Swingshift* album was the first) really brought education to me, placing it squarely where I thought I could see a space for both of us (for some reason copying the Bible passages had failed to connect). It was probably around this time that I decided to pursue a career in education, with a very loud soundtrack.

At this point music was everything, and most of everything else, too. Apart from being a musician, teaching stood out as a real job, although the fact I didn't know anyone who had actually attended university (I certainly didn't *know* the schoolteachers) left me believing it was not a serious option. Universities were for professors and such, and I certainly didn't know any of them. I doubt there were any in Sunshine.

My end-of-year HSC grades led to an offer from Deakin University to study education in Geelong. Thanks to the

Whitlam Government of nearly a decade prior, the only real costs I had to worry about were those of living away from home and commuting the hour or so it took to drive each day. The decision was made to defer for twelve months and work full-time with the goal being to create a fund to cover the costs associated with uni as my mother certainly was in no position to contribute on this front. For years Mum had told my brother and I that our secondary-school fees were paid for by our father's life insurance payout, though I later found that this was not true, which explained why *she* had to work full-time during those years.

I eventually got to uni and for my first teaching rounds I was assigned a Catholic primary school in Werribee, ironically in one of the same classrooms I had built a few years before during my brief stint in the building trade. I should have mentioned that my first plan had been to become a woodwork teacher and get there via the building trade, but that's another story. It was an unusual feeling to look at the walls and see the very nails I had driven in to hold the plasterboard in place. This was only an 'observation' round, so I did not actually teach the class at this stage.

Later teaching rounds included Barwon Heads and Ocean Grove primaries, where I was living at that point (second year of university). Ocean Grove involved working with well-known local teacher-cum-musician Trevor Bishop. Trevor was 33, with long blond hair and a moustache, and was known around Geelong as one of the town's favourite musicians. From the Queens Head Hotel to New Year's Eve at Thirteenth Beach or for a private party, Trevor Bishop and the Lost Cruisers guaranteed a great night of fun and dancing. He would 'rock up' (as he put it) at 9am to the school music room where a line of excited students awaited. Trevor would wipe aside his wet hair and comment that the waves that morning had been 'hot as', while the students chatted about the size and brand of board attached to his car roof. Once they were all in the room and playing away on their instruments, Trevor would describe how the staff at the Queens Head told the band that last night's show had been bigger than any of the Melbourne bands they had play there this year. 'It was hot as', he added, using the adjective with which he'd describe everything from waves to students' work.

This couldn't have been further from my own experience of primary school, and Trevor was a huge influence on me as a music teacher. His laid-back attitude made him a hit with the students and I was in my element combining my musical passions with education in a manner I hadn't previously been sure was possible. This was also an early experience of the teacher working with the students rather than using countless rules to gain compliance. Trevor was an integral part of their community, and parents also had immense respect for him. These were the days before standardised curricula and Trevor was able to teach music that the students loved and enjoyed playing.

Another teaching round took me to Spotswood, at that time a very working-class suburb—property prices have risen significantly there of late. The students in grades 3 and 4 presented a complex set of challenges. One student found himself in trouble for breaking into the school (this was not a case of a student who couldn't get enough of school, but a burglary).

Around this time I found myself covered in itching skin blemishes, which I later discovered were scabies, which I had never heard of apart from the punk rock musician with the moniker 'Rat Scabies'. Neither his music nor the condition was pleasant. The prescribed medications were ineffective and in desperation I removed the pests by spraying myself with Aerogard from head to toe.

University flew by in a haze of classrooms, smoky bars where I was either serving drinks in my part-time job or playing music up on stage and various shared houses and couches (not shared) as I found somewhere to stay, in some cases only to move out when the holiday season arrived and rents skyrocketed.

Each year, of the 120 or so of us who had commenced the education course at Deakin, ten or twenty disappeared, for various reasons deciding that teaching just wasn't for them. One of my best friends in the Education Faculty would never teach after he failed his final teaching round following a personality conflict with the presiding teacher. He was so dejected he signed up for the police force almost immediately.

After graduation the entire cohort awaited their dispatch to the boondocks, as was the case at the time. I was able to avoid sunny Swan Hill by securing myself a posting as maternity leave replacement at my old secondary school in Braybrook, with a class of thirty-six year 7 boys. Apart from having to break up the occasional fistfight in the classroom (not surprising as they were virtually sitting on top on each other), the most unorthodox of my duties involved working with a colleague who ran a 'sly grog shop', selling the alcohol in the school's science department from his desk ($18 for a two-litre bottle!).

Other teachers warned me, 'Wait 'til you see the staff meetings!' They had good reason. The principal, an aged brother, disallowed any questions during the meeting and read from prepared sheets the entire time. He was not to be seen around the school and staff needed to make appointments should they wish to speak with him.

The following year I took a teaching position at Charitz College. I was teaching music, drama, English and humanities, and was head of the Drama Department (not a particularly large faculty, it comprised myself and one or two other teachers).

Charitz College was a school of about 500 boys from upper primary to year 10 (it would later expand to include years 11 and 12) perched on a hill overlooking two Corios, the Geelong suburb and the bay. We could boast that we looked down on Geelong Grammar School, however we were also on the road to Anakie, in this case (fortunately) nothing more menacing than a small country town.

Drama was a relatively new area for me and I quickly discovered that improvised theatre, packaged as 'theatre sports', struck a chord with students (the fact that it was a popular television show at the time helped) and had enough variety to cover most of the skills we wanted to develop. The classes were fun, energetic and full of laughter as students worked on commercials for nuclear-powered cars or told a story which had to include random words called out as they went along. We would also have an 'Accent Day', when each student (myself included) was required to speak with a foreign accent for the duration of the lesson, causing considerable merriment when someone would visit the class to borrow a book or pass on a message. The Geelong Rock Eisteddfod was popular at the time and we competed with an all-male cast doing a comedy disco/heavy metal spoof which was the most popular act with audiences over the nights it ran. The all-male cast was quite a challenge, but the students' enthusiasm quelled any doubts I had and we pieced together a comedic dance routine akin to those in films such as *Flying High*.

My love of travel allowed me to run a geography unit on the

Pacific island nation of Vanuatu—which I had recently visited. This made a welcome change from studying the Kalahari Desert Bushmen, who had been in the textbook since I was a student in year 8. Cannibalism, volcanoes, pirates, isolated tribes and rare wildlife made Vanuatu an exciting topic in a pre-internet time when such places were truly exotic and little known.

The staff at Charitz were a close-knit, socially obstreperous bunch who were more sport-orientated than academic at that stage. Among them were at least three VFL footballers (and a future AFL coach) as well as a number of semi-professional soccer and basketball coaches. That professional sportsmen such as Brad Johnson (Western Bulldogs, AFL), Josip Skoko and the Didulica brothers Johnny and Joey (Australian soccer players) came from a school such as Charitz was no surprise.

Teaching at Charitz was remarkably uncomplicated. The students were tough, but also honest and open if you gave something of yourself. With an ethnic profile similar to that of Melbourne's western suburbs, the school had a high percentage of European migrants from working-class backgrounds. This was as basic as Catholic schools got and we were aware that these were students who would not get another opportunity outside of the even more rundown local government schools. There were a couple of other Catholic secondary colleges on the opposite side of town, but their fees and facilities put them into an entirely different category to us, something we wore with pride. In contrast to my previous school this one was in the charge of a short, bespectacled, balding principal, Brother Smith, who was friendly and open. When I knocked on his door to ask about obtaining leave to travel overseas during the Christmas break after my first year there, he told me to close the door behind me and take a seat. Fearing a lecture about losing valuable teaching time at the end of the year, I sat down and buckled myself in for the worst.

I was surprised to be given a list of all the things and places I should do and see while travelling and, on leaving an hour later, the question of how many days I needed to be aboard the crowded pre-Christmas aeroplanes leaving the country was met with, 'Whatever you need, this is something truly special.'

Such concern for my own benefit left me feeling so indebted to this wonderful man that I rarely missed a day of teaching in the next few years. His leadership style was brave, transparent and very much about his staff. Staff meetings involved debate on major questions, and any vote on a decision was implemented thoroughly as we all had ownership of the decision. Some staff meetings went beyond 6pm as teachers got involved in issues that they genuinely felt committed to. This created an incredibly vibrant atmosphere which no doubt influenced the growth in student numbers, and expansion to include years 11 and 12, at this point.

Br. Smith attended all union meetings and I saw him vote to go on strike ('Anything that improves the wages and conditions of my staff is a good thing,' he announced) before heading back to his office to put together a skeleton staff to cover the staff out on strike.

Knowing my inexperience as leader of the Drama Department, Br. Smith asked if I had any ideas to redress this and I suggested setting aside a day where I would visit other similar schools to talk with their drama teachers and see their programs and facilities. He immediately made this happen at least once a year for the next few years, and it provided some of the most valuable professional development I've ever experienced.

Br. Smith was replaced by another Brother, whom I shall call Berry (because, like Caesar, his staff did not come to praise him). We were sad to lose Tony Smith, but confident that under his superintendence the school had grown immensely in every way and was now in a strong position with plans for further growth in the form of a new library building.

The august Berry—a man well into his 60s possessed of a speaking voice that suggested not a plum but an entire plum tree in his mouth—quickly made it clear he could not accept his predecessor's participatory leadership style, and matters went downhill from there. His immediate goal appeared to be to put as many staff, students and parents offside as possible. He displayed an innate talent for doing just this. The situation was extraordinary, but everyone, even the long-serving vice-principal (who always reminded me of a wartime military general and was respectfully treated accordingly) was powerless to do anything.

Staff meetings quickly became chores that people avoided or got away from as soon as possible and our once bubbly, enthusiastic morale was replaced by a black humour reminiscent of *Hogan's Heroes* as Berry appeared incapable of building a relationship with anyone. Individuals and various groups met him in attempts to turn the situation around, only to return more bewildered than before. 'He says he is aware of what is happening but doesn't think it has anything to do with him,' they reported to those who still held out hope.

Student numbers plummeted over the next few years with a wealth of good schools nearby. It didn't help that nearly all our students were bussed in. Poor schools (that was us now) can hold student numbers if there's a dearth of alternatives, but

Charitz didn't have that luxury. Some of the senior staff left for greener pastures.

Berry continually refused to acknowledge that the principal had anything to do with morale, coming down hard on the matter of student uniforms. One of his responses to the challenge of the school's decline was to ask staff for written reflections on 'why Korea is important to giving us a vision of education'.

'Listen to upbeat and zingy music on the way to school if you want to improve your morale,' he told us with complete sincerity. We wondered if we were in some kind of reality show where our reactions to bizarre requests were being filmed. How were we supposed to react to Berry roller-skating around the schoolground wearing a cap with a propeller on it?

A triennial performance review in which staff vented their frustration at the loss of a great school was met with Berry's reappointment for a further three-year term, by which point most teaching staff had accepted that the only possible explanation could be that the school's closure was imminent. We were in free fall, with no safety net in sight.

Berry was replaced after his second three-year term. But student numbers had halved and some of the best staff were gone. There had also been redundancies due to declining enrolments. Morale was at rock bottom. The incredibly sociable staff still gathered out of hours, but their functions had the feel of wakes, full of dark humour and cynical commentary. The new principal was able to improve some things, but closure was announced just weeks after a fresh intake of more than 100 year 7 boys joined us.

The demise of Charitz was the most tragic experience I've witnessed at a school, yet my early years there were also career-shaping as I saw just what a powerful thing a religious-based school could be when it had selfless, courageous leadership and committed staff.

After spending more than a decade in Catholic secondary schools, it was time to find out what was happening in the rest of the education sector.

I was advised to approach one of the agencies that supplied emergency teachers to the region's many schools. Initially I agreed to go 'anywhere' in the spirit of investigation. Schools were particularly enthusiastic when they found that I was male and taught music. Many would completely adjust their program for the day so that I could take six or more music classes, viewing it as an opportunity to make up for the lack of a permanent music specialist. The lack of male teachers in some schools could make of me a somewhat isolated figure among all the females in the staffroom at lunchtime. Many students could not repress their excitement at encountering an adult male: role models were often in short supply in this division.

I would bring my guitar and teach classes current pop songs (U2, Killing Heidi) or Beatles tunes, watching the students walk down the corridor still singing afterwards. For repeat classes I had worksheets for songs like *Bohemian Rhapsody* and *Stairway to Heaven* and we'd listen, discuss and complete the sheet, identifying the instruments, arrangements and so on. With younger classes we'd draw a guitar or colour an existing drawing after a short cross-curricular session discussing how and why it worked. Unlike the secondary students I'd spent the majority of my time with, these guys punctuated the sessions with enthusiastic calls of 'Yeah' and 'Wow' and at the finish of the lesson they'd exclaim: 'That was the best!'

Emergency teaching is inconsistent, and you often had

little idea where you would be the following week and how many days' work you might have. The students were not always delighted to greet me. At one school in the Werribee area they were so uninterested, aggressive and ungrateful that I had to resist the urge to walk past the staffroom, go to my car and leave at recess! (I was later informed this was not an uncommon occurrence there.)

While umpiring a cricket match—an emergency teacher takes all subjects—at a school outside of Melton, a pupil of no more than nine or ten years of age threw his bat so far I nearly signalled 'four' before calling me every name imaginable after his stumps had been knocked over.

'He always does that,' a nearby fielder noted, and we continued the game as if it had never happened.

At another two-teacher school out the same way, I was impressed at the team attitude shown in running things smoothly. The senior students—in fact, grades 3, 4, 5 and 6 all shared the same room—would make the teacher a cup of tea and answer the phone in the adjoining office when it rang (there was no-one else to do it), writing down a message which they passed on to the teacher without distracting the entire group. If the weather was nice and the students had been doing well, the other teacher and myself sometimes decided to delay ringing the bell (it was actually a physical bell, not an electronic one) for ten minutes or so and extend lunchtime. This was a true 'country school', with not a house in sight in any direction and students who, despite their obvious isolation, were mature, independent and capable of accepting responsibility as they did at home every day of their lives.

Emergency teaching days quickly turned into weeks and terms. It was during a term replacement at Oberon South that

I informed shocked colleagues that in more than a decade of secondary-school teaching I had never spent an entire day (8.30-3.30) in the classroom, something they had done more times than they could count. At a private school in the outer western suburbs, a student of perhaps eleven years of age informed me that the Christmas song we were learning—John Lennon's *Happy Xmas (War Is Over)*—was not appropriate as it included the word 'Xmas' rather than 'Christmas'. This was a deliberate move by Lennon (and for the same reason as I had chosen it) to create a song that crossed boundaries in an inclusive manner, but clearly you can't please everyone.

On discussing this later, the teacher in the classroom next door told me, 'You can have my job if you want … I'm out of this place. If you think that's bad, you should hear what the parents complain about!'

Flemington Primary School was described as a school where music was a key subject, with something like 40 percent of its students learning an instrument, and there being three orchestras—one each in the junior (grades prep 1/2), middle (3/4) and senior (5/6) schools. This was the most extensive music program I have ever encountered in a primary school and the offer to teach music there a couple of days a week was very tempting.

Situated right between the Housing Commission flats and million-dollar-plus inner-city townhouses, the school building was a century-old double-storey solid brick construction that housed nearly every class. And the 400 or so pupils were indeed music-mad. During my first couple of days there they devoured my usual primary-school musical repertoire and called for more.

Yard duty conversations with students were sometimes along the lines of 'What's your favourite country in the world?

Of all the ones I've been to, I love France the most as the food is a class above anywhere else I've been.'

As Christmas approached, classes would often finish with students all sitting on the floor for a run-through of some of the songs we'd been learning. Students loved this though it could get a little claustrophobic as the younger classes wanted to be as close as possible to the guitar and the teacher. The sound of the third graders singing *Merry Xmas (War Is Over)* very nearly brought a tear to my eyes, particularly the chorus section sung by a children's choir on the recording, when I noticed actual tears from a girl in the front row. She was being comforted by those around her and when I asked what the reason was she explained tearfully,

'This song ... (sob) just reminds me of my grandma ... who died just ... (inaudible) ...,' at which point half the room seemed to burst into tears, including myself at the sheer emotion the music had summoned. The class must have been quite a sight, all returning to their own room wiping tears from their eyes and comforting each other.

As a teacher, the satisfaction in sharing the moment young students understand how music can affect them—openly displaying those emotions and being mature enough not to be too self-conscious as they did so—was indescribable. While it usually took me nearly an hour and a half to drive to Flemington from my home in the southern Geelong suburb of Belmont, it was worth every minute.

A return to full-time teaching came about at Mandama, a school perched on a valley slope which made much of the play area uneven for the 500 or so students. Being little more than a stone's throw from where I was living made it difficult to say no to this handy alternative to my long commute.

Not only was it close by, but the principal impressed me and continued to do so as the year progressed. He was genuinely interested in me as a teacher and a person, and spent time in every classroom implementing his own 'money maths' teaching method. What also became apparent was how he saw himself and the school's teachers as part of a broader education system. Despite being on a one-year contract, I found myself doing professional development (PD) days in primary mathematics, child welfare, and merit and equity, among others.

'This will be handy no matter what you do in the future,' he assured me as I signed on for another day of training. It was refreshing to have someone who believed in you enough to feel you were worth developing and later in the year I was forced to turn down some of these PD activities as the workload in class was picking up pace.

The merit and equity system was something completely foreign to me at this stage and my colleagues' professionalism at Mandama and Flemington primaries was testament to its effectiveness. In a nutshell, it meant that all interview panels for positions in the school had to include a merit-and-equity-trained teacher and should a candidate believe the selection process had treated them unfairly, they could appeal. Members of the selection panel were required to keep notes that adequately explained why one candidate had been preferred to another.

On arriving for the first day I was surprised to find a couple of dozen parents waiting for me. After initially wondering what I had done to upset so many, I soon saw that they only wished to welcome me and tell me how happy their son or daughter was to be in my classroom. Some of them even volunteered to assist in the classroom during the year. All of this was refreshingly new: in the secondary-school environment you can go the entire year without sighting some parents.

I had been given a wonderful class. We read stories, sang songs, played games and learnt about the wonders of the world. I revelled in this new environment and the students soaked up the music and enthusiasm I brought. Meetings and training sessions could extend many hours after class and the primary teacher attended all subject meetings. This included the science meeting, even though I was not teaching science that year. Remarkably, this was the first time I'd attended a science meeting at any school.

One sunny afternoon I was taking a sport class for a game of tee-ball, a game much like baseball but in which the ball is stationary on the top of a pole rather than thrown to the batter, removing the coordination issues some students face in hitting a moving target. Soft helmets were being worn by the batter and the backstop, although I'd twice found it necessary to ask the latter to retreat a few steps as his creeping forward to take the ball, which had rolled to the ground after the bat only grazed it, put him in danger of being hit.

As I stood in the centre of the triangle, the backstop crept forward again … The ring of the aluminium bat striking his head echoed across the valley, a sound I've never forgotten. He hit the ground before the echo had finished and I ran straight to him, scooping him up and carrying him directly to the medical office, about 50 metres away. My heart was beating so fast he seemed weightless as I carried his unconscious body into the building, my brain racing through all the possible injuries he might have sustained.

Upon my arrival at the office, the principal asked me to describe what had occurred and I ran through the sequence of events as best I could. He listened without interrupting, and assured me I had taken all necessary precautions. I returned to class, assured the students that all was going to be okay and, soon afterwards, dismissed them for the day.

The principal kept me informed via phone as the student made a full recovery despite missing a few school days. Only when I bumped into one of the school's office staff some time later (when I was no longer at Mandama) did I discover that the student's father had threatened the school with legal action and continued to vent his dissatisfaction for some time after the incident.

Shocked to hear this, I asked the office lady why I'd heard none of this and she replied, 'Mark (the principal) didn't want you to be worrying about what was going on behind the scenes ...'

Once again, here was an excellent principal doing excellent work that I wasn't even aware of. Had I known, my mind might have become preoccupied with the 'what ifs' and 'whys' of the entire episode and impacted on my teaching. I have seen cases where teachers have been accused of something and the principal laid the case out to the teacher in a manner that suggested 'guilty until proven otherwise', leading to a distraught teacher taking sick leave and doubtless struggling to teach to the usual standard. The loss of trust in such a case can have immeasurable consequences.

Portvale Secondary College (not its real name) was something else again. As working-class as you could get, the school of around 1000 students comprised almost entirely of portable classrooms was arranged as impressively as any maze I'd ever encountered. At the centre of the maze the staff offices—from which laptop computers were frequently stolen—lent the place the feel of a military bunker.

One imagined the secret order being issued in a breathless whisper: '*You see if you can make it to T Block. I'll cover you and call for reinforcements if we come under fire.*'

This may have been a slight exaggeration, but the sensation was real. Coming from Mandama's grade 3/4 class, where I would have had students in tears if I'd so much as raised my voice (I think it happened once in an entire year), I was really not prepared for this dramatic change of atmosphere.

On my first day I found that my seventeen-pupil year 9 English class was also occupied by ten adults. Being from a mainly private-school background where I'd never had more than one teacher's aide in the classroom, I had to ask who these adults were and why they were in my class. I was quite shocked to find that these pupils warranted so many aides. Some had an aide assigned to them for the entire day, five days a week!

That wasn't the last of the surprises. Another teacher 'came clean' with me when I mentioned the poor literacy level of the above-mentioned class, disclosing that the school applied a form of streaming that neither the students nor the parents (nor, indeed, some of the teachers) were aware of. On hearing this, my initial response was a feeling of guilt at being a part of the organisation keeping this secret from the students and their parents. Some in this class believed they were doing well academically—and some had been getting good results on the third graders' work I gave them once I realised that was the standard they were at, including one (Simon) who spoke of a career in IT.

My year 9 English class was the lowest-achieving of fifteen or sixteen within the school. The very same material I had been using for my third and fourth graders the previous year was appropriate for the stronger students in this cohort. As the year progressed I became aware that they all had home lives that were television drama (often crime) scripts in themselves. Drugs, abuse, assault, under-age sexual 'activity' and neglect bordering on homelessness were all present in the room. So-called learning difficulties were the least of their problems.

Morning briefings at Portvale often felt like speeches at a wake as the rap sheet for the week was read out to waiting staff. Apart from the bad news about students and their families, there was always a list of staff comings and goings. One morning I was surprised to hear a positive report of a graduation night function. Well, up to a point …

'We're pleased to report that the year 12 graduation night proved to be a wonderful end to the year for our senior students, their families and staff, with dancing, good food and much revelry being reported by all at the community centre … before the fire.'

For the last month or two of the year I had to move Wednesday's and Friday's year 9 English class to the un-charred half of the classroom, a new low in my teaching career. Needless to say, students were not keen to sit at blackened desks and the message sent by a school administration which determined they would continue to use this room was not lost on them.

Getting back to the first term, I immediately dispensed with as much of the year 9 English curriculum as I could. The whole class being at primary-school level, I had been adjusting the difficulty of the work to suit, enabling some to answer comprehension questions and do better in spelling tests, leading to a sense of achievement.

But they were blind to the fact that this achievement was years below year 9.

A few weeks into term one I announced to them one

morning: 'This school does a thing where they divide all students up into different groups, based on how good they are at subjects like English.

'There are some classes which have all of the students who are really good at English, some which have students of medium ability, and some with the rest of the English students.'

A hand shot up from the somewhat stunned class and Simon commented: 'We're not one of the really good classes, are we?'

'No, we're not,' I replied as the room went even quieter—which was something of a rarity. But, as the importance of this sank in, so did the realisation that for once a teacher was being straight with them.

'Are we one of the middle ones?' he pleaded, with a blend of hope and sadness.

'No, unfortunately we're not one of those groups …

'We are working at present on middle-primary-school work … but here's the plan: this term it will be grade 3/4 work to make sure everyone has the basics. Term two will be grade 5 and 6 work; term three, years 7 and 8; and by term four we will be doing year 9 English.'

I was well aware this would not be an effective method to take them all from where they were to year 9, but by giving them a roadmap and telling them exactly where they were they could at least ask questions of themselves and take some control over their learning. General student behaviour throughout the school was something I found difficult to deal with. While being upfront with my year 9 class had a positive effect on some of them, it also imposed a responsibility on myself to achieve at least a measure of what I had promised. And academic achievement was something many of these students had absolutely no experience of.

Students continued to swear like drunken sailors and expected nothing more from the teachers than detentions and contempt. After-school detention class seemed to be a routine five nights a week for dozens of wayward academics, each with his own Honours degree in Street Life and each hoping to impress fellow club members with an attendance record that in any other circumstance would result in honorary life membership.

I was told the story of a teacher who had thrown a chair through a closed window before walking out of the school never to return. One colleague, Pete, seemed to have the Midas touch in this environment. He was cool and calm with the students, friendly and affable in the staffroom. It would be nearly ten years later when I read of his fate in the newspaper. He received a payout following a court case in which he detailed his breakdown after many years of teaching the school's toughest classes, despite his pleas to be transferred, backed up with medical advice of his ill health. The court was told he would never work again.

Just as my self-increased load in year 9 English was beginning to bear fruit, the school and the state told me I also had to teach *Picnic at Hanging Rock* and the other set material for year 9, substantially increasing the pressure I was already placing on myself.

I found my hands shaking on the steering wheel as I drove to school. I was not relaxed when at home with my own young children. My thoughts turned to just walking out, like the teacher in the story I had been told. I saw a doctor; he referred me to a psychologist who gave me reading material designed to help me focus on being 'in the present' when not at school.

A position for a part-time music teacher at Belmont Primary was advertised. It was a small school which just a few years prior had faced closure and, after reinventing itself, had managed to reverse this decision. The student population was perhaps 200, many housed in portable classrooms outside of the main brick building. The mood there was positive—exactly what I needed—and I could remain at Portvale three days per week with my year 9s to whom I was committed, for reasons I could not logically explain. Portvale was destroying me, causing me to question everything I knew about teaching, even my capacity and will to keep doing it. Belmont could not have come at a better time.

It was blessed with an excellent principal, yet another Mark, who greeted every student and parent as they entered school in the morning. He knew the names of every staff member's partners and children. He wanted to know who you were. The mood in the staffroom lifted when he entered. There was a genuine sense of everyone being part of a team. He also made a point of teaching every class in the school at least once a term, when the classroom teacher really needed a break for professional or personal reasons. In short, he made everyone feel that they were important and their opinion mattered.

It was refreshing to feel a part of a positive team again. In the long term it probably saved my career, and possibly a good deal of my sanity. The contrast between the two schools I spent my week at couldn't have been greater. There was the usual lack of male teachers, meaning that some classes were excited to see me for that reason alone, but that also gave me a greater sense of purpose, knowing that for some of these young men and women you were one of the few male role models in their lives.

And I took this role of introducing music as a healthy outlet and influence in their lives very seriously.

Mark asked me to organise a Christmas celebration Mass for the school students in the church across the road. When I realised that the date was not one of my Belmont workdays, he offered me an entire day's pay for just a morning of work. After the Mass I held extra music classes in the afternoon rather than take the rest of the day off, simply to repay and in some way replicate the goodwill Mark had generated throughout the school. It was truly infectious. Everything in teaching is about goodwill. It is the things that a teacher, or principal, doesn't have to do but does anyway, that make a real difference. Anybody who thinks otherwise is kidding themselves or lacks the skills and dedication to make it happen.

The next decade and a half saw a return to the private-school system and I witnessed the accelerated tempo of the standardisation push, an experience shared by almost all schools in the country, and in many other countries. As a teacher who liked to tailor lessons to individual classes, watching schools focus everything on an ATAR score at the expense of all else, and of those students not in the market for a particular ATAR, posed a towering challenge, even at a time when I had little idea of the real consequences this change would usher in.

Judging a school, a teacher, a book, or a test on the basis of whether it's sufficiently 'rigorous' is like judging an opera based on whether it contains enough notes that are really hard for the singers to hit.

— Alfie Kohn

THE SMELL OF NAPLAN IN THE MORNING

Testing 'is a good servant but a bad master'.
— Pasi Sahlberg, Finnish Lessons 2.0, 2015

The headlines are hard to miss: *'Why up to half of all Australian teachers are quitting within the first five years', 'Naplan writing test is 'bizarre'...', 'The world's best teacher doesn't care about test scores', 'ATARs losing relevance for university admissions but students still hooked', 'Teachers are more depressed and anxious than the average Australian'.*

These are all real headlines. They point to recognition that what we are doing in our schools at present is not working and has not done so for some time.

It was in the midst of this that I visited schools in Finland, speaking with students, teachers and the teachers' teachers in Helsinki and Tampere (a couple of hours north of Helsinki) where I found that all of the above trends were virtually unknown to them.

When I explained how frequently NAPLAN[1] tests are administered in Australian schools, they asked incredulously, 'So your students have five lots of matriculation-type exams by the time they finish school?... Starting at EIGHT YEARS OLD?!'

They stared at me as though I were a child molester. In Finland children don't start school until the age of seven. They do not do any form of standardised testing until they are in their late teens.

In a recent discussion with one of my year 8 classes about growth mindset thinking—the premise that learning can help make us smarter—a third of students admitted that the experience of taking the grade 3 NAPLAN test (as eight- or nine-year-olds) had made them decide that they were 'no good' at mathematics. Some said they could actually remember making that decision. I couldn't help but wonder, 'How many of you have experienced similar moments with English and science (the other subjects tested in NAPLAN)?'

The nature of the NAPLAN test is that it presents progressively more difficult problems for the child to

---

1   The National Assessment Program—Literacy and Numeracy (NAPLAN) is an annual national assessment for all students in years 3, 5, 7 and 9. All students in these year levels are expected to participate in tests in reading, writing, language conventions (spelling, grammar and punctuation) and numeracy.

solve, until they eventually can go no further with that particular activity.

Children of this age naturally assume that if the problem is on the test, then there is an expectation that they will be able to do it. And they certainly want to please the adults, don't they? Those who raised their hands were not the rebellious students, they were mainly girls—good students who are (and certainly were at the time of sitting the test) very keen to please their parents and teachers.[2]

They trust, or at least trusted, adults and teachers unconditionally.

Finnish teachers asked me why Australian teachers let this happen to our students. It is a major discussion. How to explain why so much autonomy has been taken away from teachers (and also from administrators)? However, thinking about the obvious damage done to many young children forced to sit NAPLAN examinations, it is clear that if teachers do not speak up for the children, no-one else will. The companies that prepare the tests make many millions of dollars from them; we won't be hearing much criticism from that corner. The states themselves and school principals are reluctant to be seen as

---

2   Educational neuroscientist Dr Jared Cooney Horvath explains how long periods of stress (as a third or fifth grader might see the NAPLAN tests) impact learning. Cortisol, the stress hormone that kills neurons in the hippocampus, has free rein to damage our gateway to memory. This withers away our ability to access previously formed long-term memories, and makes it difficult to learn new information. Cooney gives the example of being trapped somewhere with no possibility for escape (a possible scenario for us in primitive times); in this situation it makes a lot more sense to block out as much of the negativity as possible and simply survive until the ordeal is over. This is what the long-term stress response does: it helps prevent memories from forming during helpless situations. (Horvath, 2019)

unsupportive, hence they are called out as trying to hide 'poor performance' and end up losing students and funding.

So who is looking at the tests and asking if they are in the best interests of the students?

In defence of teachers, when NAPLAN was first introduced it was not deemed a 'high stakes test'. Phrases such as 'a snapshot' and 'an indicator' were bandied about, the point being that teachers were not aware that what they were introducing could become a stress-inducing test which could alter for the rest of their lives students' attitudes to vitally important school subjects.

One does not have to be in Finnish schools for long to understand that educators there are true professionals. They are trusted to devise the required curriculum; national curriculum guidelines are minimal and there is no 'inspection' associated with this. Teachers are expected to devise all forms of assessment; there is no standardised testing whatsoever.

The education union is the professional body and membership is around 95 percent. It is involved in all aspects of education.

A recent report in the UK's *Guardian* newspaper spoke of the flood of interest in Finland's education system: every year hundreds of delegations comprising teachers and policymakers from all over the world pour into Helsinki to see this nirvana for themselves.

So popular has it become that international visits are strictly regulated and have to be paid for: a presentation costs €682 (£588 as at November 2019) per hour and a school visit €1240. (Weale, 2019)

Back in Tampere, I did not dare mention that the school I work at (like most other secondary schools) also has two rounds of examinations (on top of the NAPLAN ones in years 7 and 9) in each of years 9, 10 and 11, meaning students sit no fewer than 12 rounds (each 'round' could be a period of up to two or three weeks comprising examinations and study time preparing and revising for the big day) of examinations from grade 3 through to year 12.

And I nearly forgot the AGAT (the ACER General Ability Test, ACER being the Australian Council for Educational Research). This is designed to help teachers assess learning potential and aptitude in years 2 to 10. Finland makes do with only the final matriculation exam.

'Does it work?' they asked, unable to suppress their shock.

The answer was a simple 'No.'

'Well, why do they do it? Why does the teacher allow the students to do it?'

The last question really hit home. There is no reasonable answer other than to say that this is the way we have always— well, at least for the last decade and a half—done things, which seemed terribly inappropriate even as the words left my mouth. I wanted to be able to say that when the test helps us to identify students who have a weakness in their learning we are then able to provide suitable support to enable them to overcome this and continue succeeding in their education.

But this would have been a lie.

The truth is that when weaknesses are identified through NAPLAN testing there is no set policy for addressing the issue. In fact, we (well, the My School website) will encourage parents to remove their sons and daughters from the poorly performing schools (or not to send them there at all) by making the schools' results public.

The suggestion appears to be that the resultant drop in

student numbers and public shaming will somehow encourage the poorer-performing schools to 'lift their game'. That school funding is based on student numbers ensures that the poorer-performing school will also be punished financially. Parents in a position to move their children will do so, but what of those who cannot afford the money or time to relocate them to a more distant school? They remain in a classroom where many of their peers have also not done so well on the NAPLAN test.

In a school whose funding has been cut and whose better teachers are probably feeling somewhat disillusioned by all of the above, they—like the better-off parents—will be looking out for another school if possible.

If there is little to be gained by students in the NAPLAN test, then how do their teachers and principals fare? One can only imagine the stress of being principal at a school with the lowest NAPLAN score in its town or city.

Public shaming, likely loss of student numbers and funding, parent responses and students (not to mention their school) labelled the 'worst' in town. All for a standardised testing system that really does no favours for the students, who are almost certainly from the most disadvantaged part of town. Feeling somewhat guilty, I stayed silent on the fact that not only were we administering world record numbers of tests, but we were also teaching towards these tests, making their content the curriculum and judging the merits of entire schools, teachers, principals and individual students according to the results they yield.

Teachers in Australia are trained in the 'mandatory reporting' of anything resembling child abuse in any form. How could we have done this to so many thousands of students?

How many students and adults now loathe mathematics,

science or English (perhaps there is a bright side to the fact that NAPLAN omits the arts!) because of early NAPLAN experiences? If the one third of the class I asked the question to are indicative, we are talking many thousands of students.

I have often compared the obsession with increased NAPLAN-styled testing to presuming you could change the temperature by looking at the thermometer more frequently.

The discussion rarely turns to *why* we should expect improvement. Indeed, the only logical reason to expect any is that schools are now teaching *for* the NAPLAN tests, effectively making them the curriculum (at the expense of many far more useful faculties such as creativity). The fact that results are still not improving should be a cause for further concern.

According to a study published in the *Australian Journal of Language and Literacy* reporting a survey of more than 200 year 7 and 9 teachers across NSW in 2017, 'nearly 60 percent disagreed with the statement that NAPLAN provides important information on the literacy skills of students'.

'NAPLAN's out of control,' said Chris Presland, president of the NSW Secondary Principals' Council: 'The problem with it goes beyond teaching to the test, there's certainly an over-obsession with data and pressure on schools to perform because of the comparative nature of the data.'

A visit to a bookshop, educational supply store or even the local newsagent will reveal dozens of different publications all designed to improve a student's NAPLAN (National Assessment Program—Literacy and Numeracy) result. Whether any of the material tested by NAPLAN is of value to students is never debated, but it is now, by default, part of the curriculum. In April 2018, MIT professor emeritus Les Perelman undertook a comprehensive review of the NAPLAN writing test and concluded it was 'by far the most absurd and the least valid of any test that I've seen.'[3]

Why has it taken a visiting American professor to tell us this?

The US has seen similar results with its national testing program; after a decade-plus of the NCLB (No Child Left Behind) test, results indicate no changes in the 'achievement gap between poor and wealthy students and gains on achievement tests are small, even after extensive time has been allocated in schools across the nation for direct preparation for the tests'. (David C.Berliner, 2014)

In Victoria, the My School website appears to suggest that one of the main criteria for selecting a school should be NAPLAN results. The system encourages students to move from lower NAPLAN-scoring schools as if this will magically improve educational outcomes. As previously mentioned, the students remaining in the lower-scoring schools will supposedly somehow have any deficiencies identified by the test rectified by means unspecified. This is an unlikely outcome as the school concerned will most likely forfeit some of its funding through loss of student numbers and quality teachers who may have elected to move elsewhere rather than continue in the environment of a school depleted of funding and its most talented students.

---

3   Despite this, I am aware of at least one school (and I've no doubt there are many others) which has developed rubrics based on the very same NAPLAN language analysis test Prof. Perelman was referring to in a case of not only allowing NAPLAN to dictate the curriculum (which it was never designed to do and it has never been suggested was an appropriate approach to take with it) but actually taking the worst elements of NAPLAN and introducing them into the mainstream curriculum.

In Australia it can be difficult to find an educator who is not caught up in the standards movement—though I suspect many are not there by conscious choice.

The movement is, at its core, the idea that the best we can do is ensure every student has a minimum standard of certain skills. Apparently, it follows that if they have these skills they can work out the rest from there. I have witnessed situations where teachers have worked countless hours trying to fit the government-recommended curriculum into the allotted hours for a given subject, only to be told that the entire subject had been scrapped by the school or, worse, that much of the content was now deemed unnecessary as it was not relevant to the VCE examination (and therefore the ATAR score) component of the subject.

A recent report from libertarian think tank the Centre for Independent Studies pushed back against criticism of NAPLAN, stating: 'A test cannot be blamed for a lack of improvement—this would be analogous to blaming a thermometer for a hot day or criticising scales for a lack of weight loss.' (Joseph, 2018) The report at no point addresses exactly how looking at the thermometer (or scales) with greater frequency can improve results. The assumption is maintained that if we teach the 'basics', whatever they may be, creativity and all other necessary capacities will follow.

Acclaimed educationalist Sir Ken Robinson addresses this need for the basics. 'The old systems of education were not designed with this world in mind. Improving them by raising conventional standards will not meet the challenges we face now.' (Robinson, 2015)

NAPLAN suits politicians and administrators for whom it is expedient to make sweeping generalisations about the education system, students or teachers to justify spending or cuts to spending.

Finnish educator Pasi Sahlberg recently spoke of the problems of standardised testing in Australia: ' ... wherever standardised tests are running the show it narrows the curriculum and it kind of changes the whole role and meaning of going to school from general useful learning into doing well in two or three subjects. And it often makes teaching and learning very boring when the purpose is to figure out the right answer to a test.' (Pasi Sahlberg, 2018)

The NAPLAN test, a supposed 'snapshot' of the entire country's students in the same week, does little to encourage hard work and diligence in students. Instead it confronts them with challenges for which they have not had the opportunity to prepare. They do not know which elements of mathematics, English or science will be tested (although this does not prevent the detailed study of material like that contained in previous NAPLAN tests). Essentially this sends the message that, while it may identify 'naturally talented' students, nothing else— determination, persistence, grit, the 'growth mindset' and so on—matters.

The modern roots of the standards system lie with US President George W. Bush and his 2001 *No Child Left Behind Act*. It supported standards-based education reform based on the premise that setting high standards and measurable goals could improve individual outcomes in education. The Act required US states to develop assessments in basic skills. To receive federal school funding, states had to give these assessments to all students at select grade levels. This involved all students sitting a test each year.

Bush's unpopular program was followed in 2010 by Barack

Obama's *Race to the Top* program, essentially doubling down on the same shaky ideas, as if somehow tightening up the components could alter the outcomes. It increased the stress on testing, meaning that now not only would schools and governments be held accountable for results, but teachers could be given a bonus for 'excellent' results or even fired if students' results were not deemed satisfactory. This unleashed a witch-hunt-like fervour for attacking teachers (American teachers are already among the most poorly remunerated in the developed world), epitomised by a *Newsweek* cover story declaring: 'We must fire bad teachers'.

GERM WARFARE

Sahlberg has dubbed this mania for standardisation the Global Education Reform Movement (GERM for short) and is obviously dedicated to wiping out what he regards as a menace to the world's educational wellbeing. Of course, if you take the fetish for more testing, more standardisation and study theory to its extreme, good test results *can* be obtained, as South Korea, with one of the world's highest secondary-school graduation rates, has discovered. School there starts at eight in the morning and continues until nine in the evening, when most students head to private tutoring academies known as *hagwons* for an hour or two before going to bed and repeating it all the following day (a law has been passed limiting the hours *hagwons* can operate until no later than 11pm; and a dedicated police squad regularly raids *hagwons* suspected of breaking this law). *Hagwon* teachers can earn enormous salaries and it is common for families to go into debt paying fees for this private tuition. The best known of these, Andrew Kim, takes in a whopping US$4 million a year lecturing to some 150,000 students online at the equivalent of US$3.50 an hour, in addition to writing hundreds of books, textbooks and workbooks.

'In Korea, your education can be reduced to a number,' a South Korean student told Amanda Ripley while she was researching her book *The Smartest Kids in the World*. 'If your number is good, you have a good future.'[4]

Students absolutely loathe the system (although they seem to loathe the mainstream education system even more), possibly because the teachers in the latter are under great pressure to maintain student numbers—indeed their entire wage depends on it—so they administer a perpetual series of annual tests, the results of which determine entrance into the top universities, thus ensuring success in career and later life. Many believe *hagwons* are the key to South Korea's vaunted PISA scores. The world's highest-paid teacher, Andrew Kim voices great discomfort at the inequity of the system, despite profiting immensely from it himself.

'I don't think this is the ideal way,' he told Ripley. 'This leads to a vicious cycle of poor families passing on poverty to their children.' He added that, in his opinion, Finland's was a much better model to follow.

Kim said he planned to work in teacher training from 2017 (Ripley's book was published in 2013) and to improve

---

4   Interestingly, it is unlikely that someone like Charles Darwin would have achieved an impressive score in today's test formats: 'So poor in one sense is my memory that I have never been able to remember for more than a few days a single date or line of poetry.' He continues, 'What is far more important, my love of natural science has been steady and ardent.' (Duckworth, 2017)

the mainstream system for his then 6-year-old son. Ripley said that she didn't find anyone, including the head of the South Korean education system, who thought they had a good system in place, despite the country's impressive PISA results.

The case of a teenage student named Ji who murdered his mother to prevent her attending a parent-teacher night and seeing his results (which were actually quite good, but she was incredibly demanding) drew attention to this system, and much public sympathy for Ji from many South Koreans who understood the pressures a student faces in that country. (Ripley, 2013)

India recently experienced a number of suicides for the same reasons: 'TWENTY students have died by suicide in India this past week after the Board of Intermediate Education (BIE) announced their exam scores. The *Khaleej Times* reports the exams have been marked in controversy after there were discrepancies in the results.' Nearly 1 million students took the exams between February and March, and nearly 350,000 failed, causing widespread protests from parents, student groups and political parties. One student named Sirisha failed biology and set herself on fire at her home in the Narayanpet district on Saturday after her parents went out to the fields, according to the *Khaleej Times*. On Thursday, Chief Minister K. Chandrashekhar Rao ordered the recounting and re-verification of the answer sheets of all students who failed and urged them not to die by suicide, adding failing the tests didn't mean the end of their lives. (David Aaro, 2019)

The pressure to perform academically is also high in Japan, with reports that in 2014, for the first time, the most common cause of death of Japanese aged 10 to 19 was suicide.

According to the cabinet office, September 1 is historically the day when the largest number of children under 18 take their own lives. Of the 18,048 children who killed themselves between 1972 and 2013, on average 92 did so on August 31, spiking to 131 on September 1 and reverting to 94 on September 2. September 1 is the start date for the second semester of the school year. In addition to the competitive nature of Japanese education and society in general, 'The bigger issue is the competitive society where you have to beat your own friends'.

Sahlberg has a very different take on this type of competition for grades: 'Many people think that in today's highly competitive and fast-changing era, children need to learn how to compete and become winners. However, my point is the opposite. The best way for students to adapt to competition and change is to teach them to cooperate, because in such a complex and ever-changing environment, creativity and adventurousness are more necessary, and these qualities can be nurtured and born only in an environment that encourages cooperation. So as an educator, I would not encourage students to study for the sake of competition and to win. On the contrary, I want to give them a relaxed and cooperative environment so that they will have the precious qualities and opportunities to make mistakes as well that they need to face challenges in the future.' (Sahlberg, https://pasisahlberg.com, 2018)

Pasi Sahlberg is aware of the stress problem related to Australia's standardised NAPLAN tests: 'I heard some teachers telling how children are experiencing stress-related crying, vomiting and sleeplessness over the high-stakes standardised tests.'

In September 2018 news surfaced at a government inquiry of a Canberra fifth-grade student attempting to take his own life during a NAPLAN test. Reports detailed how Shane Gorman, the principal of Wanniassa High School in the capital's south, said a teacher had found the student attempting suicide in the schoolground after walking out of class during a NAPLAN test.

'People don't realise the stress it puts on kids,' Mr Gorman told an ACT inquiry into standardised testing. 'Indeed, principals across the country are reporting a rise in incidents of mental illness, particularly anxiety in students which the schools are not resourced to deal with.' (Cook, 2019)

In a move that hopefully signals the start of a shift in attitude to the GERM in Australia, the ACT Government established the inquiry into standardised testing to 'examine its effectiveness and how it affects the mental health of students as well as the morale of teachers, as part of a push to change how data from those tests is reported'.

Mr Gorman said the student walked out halfway through the test—leaving a note—and then went to take his own life.

'He was going to end it,' Mr Gorman said.

Mr Gorman appeared alongside the ACT's education union secretary Glenn Fowler, who told the inquiry public reporting of NAPLAN data caused stress for students.

'If doctors said, in near unanimity, that a practice did more harm than good for their patients, would they be ignored for nine years?' Mr Fowler said.

'NAPLAN data should be removed from the My School website now and in perpetuity.' (Evans, 2018)

Without being overly dramatic here, it is worth remembering that the Australian Capital Territory is the smallest (in size and second smallest in population) state or territory in Australia and the only reason this case was brought to public attention is that the ACT held an inquiry into standardised testing.

The conclusions of this and other inquiries into NAPLAN

and standardised testing will need to find a way around the Australian Council for Educational Research which administers, monitors and creates the materials for NAPLAN. For reasons many find obvious, it cannot be expected to oppose a system of which it is such an integral part.

I contacted ACER to ask about its NAPLAN review methods. There was no response. Their website makes it clear that their focus is on educational measurement: 'Our mission is to create and promote research-based knowledge, products and services that can be used to improve learning across the lifespan.'

It is a mystery that an educationalist of the standing of Pasi Sahlberg should be resident in Australia working at the University of New South Wales and as an adviser to the Gonski Institute yet not have any role to do with ACER.

It (NAPLAN) just wouldn't work in our (Finnish) system. Stressed kids are not learning and stressed teachers are not teaching. I wish and hope [Australia] provides more room for teachers to do more of the stuff that teachers do best and remove a lot of the rote and mechanical assessments and grading papers.

— Linda Liukas, Finnish education author

NOT A FIGHT TO THE FINNISH

We want our teachers to focus on learning, not testing. We do not, at all, believe in ranking students and ranking schools ...

In Finland, having happy children is the most important thing, we want to bring back the joy of learning. When you go to schools here, you see happy, active and engaged pupils.

— Kristiina Volmari from the Finnish National Agency for Education

The Finnish system values learning (both the verb and the noun), not grades. A specific memory I have from discussions with Finnish educators is being asked the question, 'Why are Australian teachers so obsessed with *grades*?'

It was this question that led me to query why teachers such as myself had—for I could not dispute this—come to equate 'grades' with education and learning. We had somehow decided that one thing was the other. Now initially this seems to be a harmless, minor issue of semantics. But what message is it giving students? Are the Finnish gaining something through keeping 'grades' out of learning and education as much as possible? Are we sending a message that it is not learning (verb) that is important? Through questions such as this I began to see that what the Finnish were accomplishing had more to do with attitude than 'technique' or 'method'.

In Finland, assessment is the tiny piece tagged onto the end of a unit of work which may aid teaching and understanding of the student—and it does not take the form of a percentage grade. I say 'may' here because the form an assessment takes is at the discretion of the teacher, and will vary from class to class and teacher to teacher.

The Finnish teachers know nothing of figures suggesting that half of all teachers leave the profession within the first five years (I have also seen the same figure in headlines from the US and UK). They place a high value on teachers having a life away from the classroom, keeping the hours both teachers and students spend at school to a minimum (the hours of instruction are also fewer) and ensuring that both are fresh and motivated for the next day. Homework is also kept to a minimum, for similar reasons.

Teachers are highly respected, well-paid professionals with great autonomy. A recent report in Australia found that 'Eighty percent of teachers have experienced some form of student or parent bullying or harassment over the past nine to twelve months'. (Romensky, 2019)

Finnish teachers would also be surprised to hear that over half of Australian teachers suffer from anxiety and nearly one fifth are depressed—and that around 18 percent had symptoms that met the criteria for moderate to severe depression. Nearly 62 percent met criteria for moderate to severe anxiety while just under 20 percent had severe anxiety. And more than half—56 percent—met criteria for moderately to extremely severe somatic symptoms. This is when the symptoms are physical and can include pain, nausea, dizziness and fainting. Alarmingly, 17 percent screened positive for probable alcohol abuse or dependence. (Stapleton, 2019)

It was in this environment where Finnish schools have been scoring near the top of world rankings on the PISA tests. The Finns themselves are not particularly enthusiastic about this as they place little value on standardised tests: in fact some felt that they must be doing something wrong to be up with the best in a standardised test-based assessment that measures student achievement in three academic areas (Sahlberg, Finnish Lessons 2.0, 2015). Intrigued by this, I decided to seek out some answers.

I was aware of a sense that things had not improved, that the national curriculum (the Australian Curriculum), NAPLAN, IT, the Institute of Teaching (the education sector's 'professional body') and many other 'improvements' to the profession had somehow given us no improvement at all. The headlines quoted above confirm this, as do nearly two decades of NAPLAN and PISA results.

The questions I sought answers to were:

1. Why are Australian teachers leaving the profession in such high numbers? What stories do these teachers have to tell and are there any commonalities?
2. How does the Finnish system improve student engagement and outcomes (I won't say 'results') while spending less time in class?
3. Can some of the ideas behind the Finnish methods be applied here in Australia, amid a system obsessed with standardised testing and curricula? Could the move away from the cult of standardised testing perhaps come from within the classroom, driven by teachers rather than politicians and administrators?
4. Finally, could all of the above be related, and the adoption of a more student-based system not driven by standardisation solve many of the problems causing the teacher exodus and even turn around the flatlining of student achievement witnessed over the last few decades?

If there were to be another question here it would surely have to be, 'Why isn't *everybody* asking these questions?'

In Finland, education is a public service. General education, vocational education (of which the closest equivalent in Australia might be a TAFE institute) and higher education are all free of charge. Basic education, upper secondary education and vocational education are financed by state and local authorities, general and vocational education by local authorities. In Finland, these local providers of education are basically municipalities responsible for arranging education that can set up their own local curricula with special emphasis, for example, on music or languages, while also deferring to the national core curriculum.

Writing on the American experience, Linda Darling-Hammond noted that, 'Our great university system is now the training ground for students from other countries who, unlike American students, are fully subsidised by their governments.' (Darling-Hammond, 2010)[1] The same is true of Australia's universities. Intel's director of research, Andrew Chien, noted that advanced degrees in the fields of science and engineering 'hold the keys to the kingdom in terms of unleashing what is possible in the world and driving change'.

For more than twenty years now we've been coming up with common national standards, common national tests (NAPLAN, or 'Napalm' as I like to call it: it *is* scary and can wreak long-lasting harm in the lives of those exposed to it), greater competition between schools, teachers and students (via NAPLAN and ATAR scores), a national curriculum, and more and more tests and standardised curricula. Despite all this, there has been limited, if any, improvement, and in many cases 'results' have gone backwards.

Meanwhile, politicians call for performance-based pay for teachers and principals, the closure of poorly performing schools, tougher entrance requirements for teacher training (and sometimes, contradictorily, 'easier' entrance into teacher

---

1   A recent report from the National Science Foundation notes that the pipeline into America's Ph.D. programs is now dominated by graduates from Chinese universities. In 2006, for the first time ever, the top producers of students coming into US doctoral programs were the Tsinghua and Beijing universities ... The two Chinese universities nearly quadrupled the number of students they sent to US doctoral programs over the course of a decade. (Darling-Hammond, 2010)

training as seen in the six-week course pushed by some and even featured in a recent television documentary/reality show, *Testing Teachers*), the sacking of poorly performing teachers and principals, and reports and investigations into what is going wrong in our schools.[2]

As one Finnish teacher told me, 'In Finland, *all* schools have to be good schools.'

As David C. Berliner observes, 'Competition is appropriate in some arenas, but in education it is a repugnant motivator that will alienate teachers from one another and decrease the chances of all students succeeding.' He continues, 'Competition is about winners and losers among teachers and their students. A Darwinian survival of the fittest, applied to education, cannot be healthy for an education system in a democracy.' (David C. Berliner, 2014)

Clearly, there are a lot of questions to be asked and, rather than asking politicians, I want to ask classroom teachers and principals, or those who have left the classroom, (in great numbers as the reports suggest) just what they are seeing out there in Australian schools. At best, we can find answers to some of the questions mentioned previously; at worst this book may be a caution on where the pitfalls lie for those planning to go into teaching under the current system.

---

2   As one Finnish teacher told me on this matter: 'What sounds unbelievable to my Finnish ears is all the talk about "poor-performing teachers". The reason for this, naturally, is because we don't have any tests or standardised evaluation of teachers. It would be very hard for me to even imagine where to start if someone asked me to draft a plan on how to evaluate a teacher's work results. Talking about results in the same sentence with teaching is a little complicated since the results are not always immediately visible or noticeable, but they may come later on in the life of a student.'

Finland's results have slipped because the boys spend time on and have interest in something other than school. Another reason may be that while most of the thirty-four OECD member countries [like Australia] have adjusted their education policies and designed school reforms with higher rankings in PISA in mind, Finland has done the opposite.

— Pasi Sahlberg

Secondly, some of the thinking that currently makes the Finnish education system one of the most admired in the world, while improving student and teacher outcomes, may become part of educational thinking in Australia. Government and educational administrations may be slow to respond to these ideas, but perhaps change can come from the classroom and spread upwards through the system?

Finland has found a way to maintain student 'buy-in' to the idea of education. I saw students who looked no different to those I've seen at schools in Australia—or the United States— but somehow the cynicism, boredom and frustration with the inflexible system don't seem to be present in Finnish students.

Amanda Ripley queried Kim, an American exchange student in Finland (who had obviously seen both sides of the equation) about this phenomenon. Kim told her: '… there just seemed to be something in the air here. Whatever it was, it made everyone more serious about learning, even the kids who had not bought into other adult dictates.' Kim's reference to 'other adult dictates' referred to the fact that these students were still rebelling against the adult society around them, but neglecting their education did not appear to be among their choices for this rebellion. (Ripley, 2013)

Perhaps it is the greater autonomy of the teachers: they feel they have control and responsibility for a broad segment of the students' learning and the students themselves can sense and appreciate this. I suspect this is a huge part of the equation. For both teachers and students, education is not some mass of 'content' set by faceless administrators and routinely tested as though the students were all guinea pigs in some national trial.

Education in Finland is a more personal thing, negotiated between teacher and student, and the fact that both have some input into this process creates a sense of ownership absent from many other education systems. It is human nature to appreciate the personalisation of something and rally against (or at least keep a distance from) inflexible frameworks being constructed around us. Former teacher Gabbie Stroud described one school she worked at, before things took a turn for the worse, where 'teacher opinion mattered. Suggestions made at staff meetings were considered.'[3]

Pasi Sahlberg: 'In my country we want to have teachers with self-esteem, that they feel that they are professionals just like medical doctors and lawyers and others. And if you don't

---

3   The Portuguese Government launched the Project for Autonomy and Curriculum Flexibility to enable schools to promote teaching practices that facilitate better learning and holistic skills development among students. As part of the program, schools identify student learning objectives aligned with the National Skills Strategy and student competency framework, which include 21st-century skills and cross-curricular competencies, and adapt their curriculum accordingly. Teachers and principals at the school level collaborate professionally to introduce new pedagogical approaches, interdisciplinary and cross-classroom activities aligned to these student learning objectives. The project thus promotes innovation in teaching methods at the school level, driven by educators themselves. (*TALIS - The OECD Teaching and Learning International Survey, 2019*)

have the same degree, same level of preparation for that, it's very hard ...'

In Finland, teachers are carefully chosen (this is not just a symbolic gesture: fewer than 10 percent of applicants are successful) and trained, then trusted to develop a national core curriculum, to run their own classrooms, to choose their own textbooks. School leaders and teachers, Amanda Ripley found, were free to write their own lesson plans, engineer experiments within their schools to find out what worked, and generally design a more creative system than any centralised authority could. (Ripley, 2013)

> *Most of the decisions are made at a school and classroom level. Foreign visitors and politicians say, 'Wow, it's amazing how much you trust the principals and the teachers, but for us it is kind of obvious—the ideology is "Train the teachers well and then let them be", because they know best.'*

— Kristiina Volmari

FINLAND'S EDUCATION SYSTEM—BORN OR MADE?

Historical test results show that Finnish kids were not born smart; they got that way recently. Change, it turned out, could come within a single generation. One thing that is immediately obvious in Finland is that the children are trusted and given independence and responsibility. Children under the age of 10 are walking to and from school, even in cities like Helsinki and Tampere. They are not 'wrapped in cotton wool' or driven to and from school by protective parents scared to let them out of their sight. From secondary-school age, students may find themselves at school with free time.[4] The previously mentioned American exchange student, Kim, was surprised to find she could come and go freely from her Finnish school, visit nearby shops or just take a break with other students at a coffee shop. Kim also noted that teenagers were treated more like adults: there were no regularly scheduled parent-teacher conferences. If teachers had a problem with a student, they usually just got together with the student.

To an extent this independence mirrors the autonomy given to Finnish teachers and it brings to mind an anecdote Timothy Walker related in *Teach Like Finland*. He, too, had noted young children walking great distances through the middle of Helsinki to get to and from school, when in his own country, America, children of the same age would be driven to school and sometimes escorted to the classroom door, and not allowed to leave the school until a guardian arrived to take them.

Walker put it this way: 'Finnish children … have many opportunities, at home and at school, to do things by themselves without handholding, and through these opportunities they seem more self-directed as learners.' He continued, 'Academic

---

4   There are various studies that back up these insights. One paper published last year in the journal *Developmental Psychology* found that two-year-olds whose mothers intervened more in their play ended up less emotionally resilient than children who were left to figure stuff out by themselves. 'The problem here really is that if you don't learn skills to self-regulate, how can you self-regulate when you leave the home?' said Dieter Wolke, professor of developmental psychology and individual differences at the University of Warwick, about the study. 'In a way it is a form of abusiveness—taking this opportunity away from children.' (Godwin, 2019)

literature suggests that a sense of autonomy is a major ingredient of happiness (Pinsker, 2016) and during those two years of teaching in Helsinki I saw that, too: my students seemed to thrive whenever I would make decisions to develop their agency.' (Walker, 2017)[5]

That we drown our students in rules and regulations is hard to refute. We are after all, imposing upon them a curriculum and methods of learning in which they have had no say or input. Of course we will need to use a lot of rules and regulations to keep them in line. But it does have consequences, as seventeen-year-old student Kate Simonds said in her 2015 TEDx talk: 'We're expected to raise our hands to use the restrooms, then three months later be ready to go to college or have a full-time job, support ourselves, and live on our own. It's not logical.' (Couros, 2015)

I recently witnessed a secondary-school staff meeting in Australia where debate continued for 30–40 minutes about the school's mobile-phone policy, with not a mention of student wishes or the possibility of allowing students to take responsibility for their devices as they do every day in the world outside of school. As in most Australian schools, the rules will be imposed on the students and compliance is not optional. As educationists like Sir Ken Robinson so often point out, it is this compliance with extensive rules and rubrics that

---

5   Overall, a vast majority of teachers and school leaders in Finland view their colleagues as open to change and their schools as places that have the capacity to adopt innovative practices. In Finland, 75 percent of teachers also report that they and their colleagues support each other in implementing new ideas. This is lower than the average share across OECD countries and economies participating in TALIS (78 percent). (*TALIS - The OECD Teaching and Learning International Survey, 2019*)

leaves students totally unprepared for the conditions they will find themselves in when they attend university or work in the 'real' world.

This culture of compliance is not conducive to a positive relationship between teachers and students, nor sometimes between teachers and parents. The figure 'Eighty percent of teachers have experienced some form of student or parent bullying or harassment over the past nine to 12 months' (Romensky, 2019) is no surprise in a culture where students, teachers and parents are all under intense pressure to obtain high marks on the standardised curriculum and tests. Recent developments in IT now equip schools and parents with the ability to see exactly which lesson the student should be studying at any time and how the teacher should be going about this. The implicit message here is that students, teachers and parents should all be rigidly following the set program: anything else is not acceptable. It implies that some teachers cannot be trusted and a parent ought to check up and see if they are doing 'what they are supposed to be doing'.[6] A recent report from the UK teachers' union described a similar phenomenon there, where parents are sending aggressive communications to teachers via email and 'specialist school messaging apps such as Class Dojo', often late at night, and demanding immediate attention. (Adams, 2019)

---

6   Research on the use of laptops in schools is not positive. 'Only employ technology if it is integral to the learning task. A good rule of thumb: if you can run the session or activity in person using physical tools and interaction—do it! ... However if *learning* is not your ultimate goal ... technology is a great means to boost engagement and enjoyment—though, as we learnt earlier, engagement and enjoyment are not synonymous with learning ... If it's to help others embody new ideas, then ensure the technology is essential, otherwise ditch it.' (Horvath, 2019)

This is another level of standardisation and stress placed on teachers and students. The head of a La Trobe University study, Dr Paulina Billett, said she was surprised not only by the level of bullying and harassment towards teachers, particularly in an era where society is purportedly concerned about mental health issues, but by the severe impact on teachers' lives.

'What it did to them in their family home, the depression that a lot of them actually experienced, people reporting symptoms of PTSD, things like that, that you wouldn't immediately locate in the context of teaching,' she said. (Romensky, 2019)

Compliance does not foster innovation. In fact, demanding conformity does quite the opposite. In *The Innovator's Mindset* George Couros felt this had an impact on teachers also. 'Many teachers are bored with the profession because they know there is a lot more to learning than schools have to offer today. Those teachers want to be innovative, but, instead of connecting and learning from others around the world, let alone with colleagues in their own schools, they spend their time in staff meetings that often seem irrelevant to the heart of teaching.'

Couros addresses the standardisation system: 'As leaders, if we ask teachers to use their own time to do anything what we're really telling them is it's not important. The focus on compliance and implementation of programs in much of today's professional development does not inspire teachers to be creative, nor does it foster a culture of innovation. Instead it forces inspired educators to colour outside the lines, and even break the rules to create relevant opportunities for their students … Their students remember them as 'great teachers' not because of the test scores they received but because their lives were touched.' (Couros, 2015)

It takes courage to challenge the ideas and practices that have made us successful. But, in a world that moves and changes so fast, holding on to conventional wisdom is frequently not the best option.

According to the Organisation for Economic Cooperation and Development's 2018 *Education at a Glance* report, 'In 2017 the net teaching time for Australian primary teachers per year was 865 hours, compared to the OECD average of 778 hours. Upper-secondary teachers taught 797 hours, it found, compared to the OECD average of 655.'

Australian teachers are in charge of larger classes and working significantly more hours than the OECD average, a likely factor in falling results on standardised tests and another huge difference between the Australian and Finnish systems. Anything Australian teachers may be lacking in qualifications or status they certainly make up for with increased working hours.

Finnish teachers are encouraged to lead active lives outside of teaching, and to minimise their work hours away from school to ensure that they are fresh rather than rundown when they are at school.

A recent Australian study reported in *The Conversation* found that 'practitioner-teachers—such as art teachers practising art and biology teachers observing nature—see themselves as better-quality teachers when measured against key principles of learning and teaching.'[7]

---

7   The Good School (*La Buona Scuola*) reform in Italy, introduced in 2015, made in-service training mandatory, permanent and structural. The Italian Government invested substantially to provide training in areas of school autonomy, evaluation, innovative teaching, 21st-

The researchers concluded, 'While induction and mentoring programs have supported teachers well in their first year or two, our study shows that encouraging them to practise their discipline could be a solution to retaining quality teachers long-term.' (Morris & Imms, 2019)

Regardless of the time-consuming and complex process of becoming a teacher in Finland, teaching is 'the single most desirable career choice among young Finns'. (Uusimaki, 2013)

The report also found teaching was the first-choice career for only 58 percent of teachers in Australia compared with 67 percent across the OECD countries.

Indeed, a 2014 a government report estimated that 20 percent of education graduates do not register as teachers on graduating, meaning many leave before they've even started their career.[8]

---

century skills (such as digital skills and schoolwork schemes) and skills for inclusive education. Through the program, teachers are given €500 per year on their Teachers Card to participate in training activities, purchase materials or attend conferences. Training offers are matched with training demands via a digital platform. (*TALIS - The OECD Teaching and Learning International Survey, 2019*)

8   Associate Professor Philip Riley from the Australian Catholic University, who is leading research into teacher attrition, says the first problem is that no-one is collecting and coordinating the data on a federal level. 'There are nine parallel [education] systems operating across Australia,' Prof. Riley explains. 'There's state, Catholic and independent. Each of them is collecting information in different ways, but no-one is bringing that information together.' (Stroud G., 2017)

WHAT ARE WE TEACHING?

(THE COURSE WHISPERER)

The goal of schools in Australia today is to help students earn good grades.[1] I cannot recall the last time I attended a curriculum-related meeting at a school where the question 'What constitutes a good education?', or even 'What do the students want to do and how can we best cater to their interests?' was raised. Indeed, most curriculum content questions are resolved based on how convenient (to the teachers and the

---

[1] Referring to a similar situation in business, Gary Chapman and Paul White, writing in *The 5 Languages of Appreciation in the Workplace: Empowering Organizations by Encouraging People*, observed, 'Recognition, however, does not work well when organizations try to use large organizational programs to make employees feel valued individually. In fact, this often creates negative backlash within the organization (sarcasm and resentment).' (Gary Chapman and Paul White, 2019)

school) the assessment of that particular aspect will be ('*Can we test for it or put it on a task where a rubric can be devised stating exactly what is required?*') Is it on the NAPLAN test or does it appear on the VCE examinations? Can it be included in the examination? Will the assessment task be easy to grade?

In a recent conversation concerning variety in the curriculum (i.e. where not all students are studying the same texts), a teacher colleague argued that all students have to study the same thing to ensure fairness when achievement awards are given at the end of the year! This equates to 100 percent of the students being forced to study the same texts and complete the same tests and assessment tasks so that the distribution of awards to 1 percent can be done 'fairly'. There is also the argument that it becomes essential to change the set texts every couple of years, regardless of their effectiveness or suitability, to ensure that students do not submit tasks from previous years.

That the same tasks are given repeatedly for many years running, though, generates its own set of concerns, as evidenced by the decision of New Zealand to abandon standardisation— and of Singapore to abandon age-based rankings—in favour of stimulating students to exercise an inquiring mind.

> *The Singaporean education system has an initiative called 'Thinking Schools, Learning Nation' which includes the statement: 'Thinking Schools will be the cradle of thinking students as well as thinking adults and this spirit of learning should accompany our students even after they leave school.'*
> — Darling-Hammond, 2010)[2]

---

2   Singapore sets its teachers on the path to prepare for leadership roles early in their career, through an identified leadership track. Teachers

In his book *The Global Achievement Gap*, Tony Wagner noted the lack of debate among teachers about appropriate curriculum. When he asked teachers why this was so, many said they wanted to have these conversations but felt obligated to spend the available time on covering the curriculum necessary to ensure that students would pass the standardised tests. An example of this from the current Australian Curriculum is that humanities (which incorporates the subjects history, geography, economics, politics and law) schedules the study of World War II at year 10 level. It is not compulsory for students to study humanities at year 10 level, meaning that a great many students are completing their education having never studied this event, the rise of the Nazi ideology or the Holocaust. It should be no surprise to see media outrage when the symbolism of this ideology appears in recent political contexts.

Wagner also found that 65 percent of college professors report that what is taught in high school does not prepare students for college. One major reason is that the tests students must take in high school for state accountability purposes usually measure 9th or 10th grade level knowledge and skills. Primarily multiple-choice assessments, they rarely ask students to explain their reasoning or to apply knowledge to new situations (skills that are critical for success in college) ...' (Wagner, 2014)

---

who aim to be school leaders in the future can assume specific roles and responsibilities. For new principals, the National Institute of Education in Singapore, in collaboration with the Ministry of Education, designed a six-month pre-service program called Leaders in Education. A key focus of the program is innovation and the creation of new knowledge, whereby the principal is seen as instrumental in collaboratively creating knowledge tailored to their school's context. (*TALIS - The OECD Teaching and Learning International Survey, 2019*)

While Wagner's research is from American samples, there is no reason to think it would not apply in Australia with our multiple standardised testing approaches.

A long time ago, people thought it was raw materials that drove the economy … That's not true anymore. What drives economies is the education of the people and the innovation that they can then create.

— Jeff Bezos

For decades, members of elite (and not-so-elite) sports teams all followed the same training regimes, hewing to the same warm-up activities, dietary requirements, fitness standards, skill sets, recovery routines and so on. In fact, catchphrases such as 'There's no *I* in TEAM' were commonly bandied about as subtle reminders that this idea should not be questioned. Attend an elite sports team's training session today and you will see perhaps a dozen different warm-up exercises; a different diet regime for every player; and individual fitness, skills and recovery routines for each team member based on their age, previous injuries, existing skills and so on. The modern sports coach knows that the best outcome for the team comes from optimising conditions for each individual on that team. No two players are the same, and no-one would want them to be. It's their unique individual characteristics that, when combined, create the champion team. While an Australian might argue that the classroom is not a team situation, the Finn would take a broader outlook and say students are being prepared to take their place in the outside world where they will form part of a much larger team.

The modern sports coach is also aware that the players must be 'on side' with the coach: the old style of loud, brash delivery bordering on verbal abuse common in the seventies and eighties has been replaced by emphasis on understanding the players, empathising with them and working with them to build a trust-based relationship.

Michael Poulton, who specialises in sports coach development having previously worked for the AFL and several of its clubs, has watched the shift occur. 'We've matured as an industry. The notion of, "Do as I say and don't ever question it" and "Don't think, just do" is not contemporary thinking,' Poulton said.

'People aren't striving to be their best when they're just being told, "This is the way to do it, everyone does it that way so shut up and keep going."

The big thing is around the understanding of yourself— and that does take time—and *What impact do I have on other people?*'

The change that has occurred in the last few decades in sports culture is the same one that is needed in Australian education. At present we are obsessed with everyone doing the same thing, essentially because it is convenient for educators and politicians, much as it was convenient for the sports coach decades ago.

Darling-Hammond, Bransford et al. (2005) began this process in their vision for classroom management. Classroom management encompasses many practices integral to teaching, such as developing relationships; structuring respectful classroom communities where students can work productively; organising productive work around a meaningful curriculum; teaching moral development and citizenship; making decisions about timing and other aspects of instructional planning; successfully moving children to learn; and encouraging parent involvement.

Sir Ken Robinson has a lot to say about this idea of *the standard*, beginning with the obvious '... people don't come in standard versions—and, when it comes to the curriculum itself, 'Only some areas of education lend themselves to being standardised'. As mentioned earlier, it might be easier to say that some areas of education are easier to assess than others, and since assessment is the focus of the standards obsession, those areas that do not lend themselves to this will fall from favour. The result is a much narrower curriculum, which brings with it another set of issues.[3]

CREATIVITY

'The first victims of the standards obsession will invariably be the arts, the appreciation of which has always been a somewhat subjective matter. Indeed, this extends to any area where imagination and creativity are options. If you run an education system based on standardisation and conformity that suppresses individuality, imagination and creativity, don't be surprised if that's what it does.'

Robinson also recognises the impact this type of thinking has on students who do not fit into the subject areas favoured by the standards system: '... many highly talented, brilliant people think they're not because the thing they were good at in school wasn't valued or was actually stigmatised.' (Robinson, 2015)

---

3   'The notion was that one could organize all of the facts needed into a set body of knowledge and divide it up neatly into the 12 years of schooling, doling out the information through graded textbooks and testing it regularly.' (Darling-Hammond, 2010)

It is not only the students' creativity that has suffered. Teaching once attracted creative individuals who could inspire their students by forging creative teaching strategies and curriculum development. In my own years of pupillage it was a teacher developing a student-produced school newspaper that first allowed me to write on the topics I was passionate about. This would not be encouraged in today's VCE environment as the pressure to achieve the highest possible ATAR score is all-encompassing. Students would simply not have time to contribute to school newspapers, and the writing done in today's school is on topics unlikely to appear in the VCE examination. Yet, looking back, it is clear that the school newspaper was to have far greater influence on my life than any of the grades I achieved.

In 2012 Pasi Sahlberg asked Finnish teachers what it would take for them to leave their chosen profession. Salary was rarely mentioned but one of the most popular responses was that if they were to lose their autonomy within the school and the classroom, their career choice would come into question. (Sahlberg, Finnish Lessons 2.0, 2015)

A 'professionally run' school in Australia will have every week's learning in each subject area mapped out according to the prescribed Australian Curriculum guidelines, along with the expected standards each student should be attaining. A teacher who fails to do this or fails to have their class at the prescribed point in Week 8 (for example) of the semester may be deemed unprofessional. A teacher who so much as veers away from the prescribed curriculum or gives students a different test or task to that set down in the curriculum may also find themselves labelled unprofessional, non-team players. Effectively, the creative teachers have been stifled, their methods criticised and the creative subjects marginalised as those all-important tests take priority.

Given the current system described above, it is only natural to ask, *Where can innovation or improvement possibly occur?*

In the Finnish system, where the trainee teacher is asked to learn the 'best practice' and then develop another, even better way, innovation is constantly happening. One of the most difficult aspects of trying to 'mine' the Finnish system is the fact that it is constantly evolving. This is its strength. The traditional education system, with its roots in the Industrial Revolution, had good reason for the ideas that drove it. 'These systems were developed in large part to meet the labour needs of the Industrial Revolution … on the principles of mass production … The problem is that these systems are inherently unsuited to the wholly different circumstances of the 21st century.' (Robinson, 2015)

> *It's a gift if you can keep your childlike sense of wonder, and it helps with creativity. It helps to have fun.*
>
> — Jeff Bezos

Many of the occupations present-day students will be engaged in have not yet been conceived of, but the leaders of some of the world's most innovative companies have made it known that they want cutting-edge, creative staff who are adaptable[4] and able to come up with new ideas.

As a way of improving efficiency, Elon Musk recently instructed his staff to 'Walk out of a meeting or drop off a call

---

4   At a recent forum in Melbourne, 'How would you re-imagine education?' with Harvard professor Eric Mazur, a representative from the SEEK employment agency stated that adaptability was the

as soon as it is obvious you aren't adding value. It is not rude to leave, it is rude to make someone stay and waste their time.' Many organisations, including schools, now have 'meeting expectations', a list of patronising rules to be followed in meetings that effectively stifle real debate and questioning by not allowing for critical analysis. This takes me back to my time in Finland when teachers asked me why we (Australian educators) continued to use standardised testing and curriculum despite the fact that they were clearly not leading to improvements. I doubt they'd have been impressed if I had added that we are not allowed to question such things, let alone use our 'autonomy' to instigate change.

Returning to curricular matters, American worldwide management consulting firm McKinsey and Company has found: 'The hardest activities to automate with currently available technologies are those that involve managing and developing people (9 percent automation potential) or that apply expertise to decision making, planning, or creative work (18 percent).' (McKinsey and Company, 2016)

> *The fun of play, particularly playing games, is developing resilient, adaptive strategies to respond to unpredictable events.*
>
> — Steve Johnson

Thomas Friedman put it this way: '… any job—blue- or white-collar—that can be broken down into a routine and transformed into bits and bytes can now be exported to other countries where there is a rapidly increasing number of highly educated

---

one quality employers sought, and struggled to find in the current generation entering the workforce.

"knowledge workers" who will work for a small fraction of the salary of a comparable American worker.' (Friedman, 2005) As in America, so goes Australia. Already our country has outsourced much of its manufacturing and call-centre work, and that is just those companies that haven't completely closed down or moved their entire operation offshore.

Friedman goes on to remind us that we can include jobs in architecture, engineering, software code-writing, technical support specialists, customer services, accountants ... jobs that rely on the skilled use of data and information that can now easily be sent, received and processed instantaneously anywhere in the world. Anyone who has tried to get tech support for their phone or computer of late will be familiar with this. The countries these people live in are increasingly producing workers well versed in the education 'basics' and keen to take part in the lifestyles of the Western economies Australians and Americans take for granted.

Apart from not equipping students for the world in which they will seek employment, the obsession with standards leaves those students whose talents are in the arts and other creative pursuits feeling that they have no value, and they may even be labelled slow. (Robinson refers to '... the deadening effects of testing and standardisation on them, their children, or their friends'.) While careers such as journalism may to an extent be taken over by automation and computers, the writing of humorous, creative, sarcastic or ironic pieces will always be the domain of an intelligent, talented, imaginative human writer.

Tony Wagner was on to the inappropriateness of much of our current curriculum for dealing with modern life when he wrote: '... work, learning and citizenship in the twenty-first century demand that we all know how to *think*—to reason, analyse, weigh evidence, problem-solve—and to *communicate effectively*. They are no longer skills that only the elites of a society must master; they are essential survival skills for all of us.'[5]

Wagner continues: '(Students) memorize names and dates in history, but they cannot explain the larger significance of historical events ... they are required to memorize (and usually quickly forget) a wide range of scientific facts, but very few know how to apply the scientific method—how to formulate a hypothesis, test it, and analyse the results.' (Wagner, 2014)

Similar learnings are observed in mathematics. Overall, effective communication, critical thinking skills and curiosity are often absent from the current curriculum.

Robert Nelson, associate director of student experience at Monash University, has written about the difficulty in teaching creativity, noting that some of the paralysis arises because you can't easily define creativity. It resists the measurement strategies that we're familiar with.

It might be satisfying to craft models for such analytical processes, as is often the case in classroom settings, but they distort the natural, wayward flux of imaginative thinking. Often, it is not about solving a problem but *seeing* a problem that no-one else has identified.

---

5   'Whereas in 1967 more than half (54%) of the country's [the United States'] economic output was in the production of material goods and delivery of material services (such as transportation, construction and retailing), by 1997 nearly two thirds (63%) was in the production of information products (such as computers, books, televisions, and software) and the provision of information services (such as telecommunications, financial services, and education). Information services alone grew from about one third to more than half of the economy during that 30-year period.' (Darling-Hammond, 2010)

The standards system once again stifles creativity, as Nelson points out: 'Because creativity in essence is somewhat irresponsible, it isn't easy to locate in syllabus and [is] impossible to teach in a culture of learning outcomes.

Learning outcomes are statements of what the student will gain from the subject or unit that you're teaching. Internationally and across the tertiary system, they take the form of: "On successful completion of this subject, you will be able to …" Everything taught should then support the outcomes and all assessment should allow the students to demonstrate that they have met them.' (Nelson, 2018)

The amount of knowledge available to the individual today is astounding.[6] YouTube alone contains more than 5 billion videos, with an additional 300 hours of content being added every minute. All of these contain information of some sort. There are nearly 2 billion websites and more than 51 percent of the planet's population access it with some regularity.

To give a specific example of how this has changed accessibility and the value of knowledge, let me relate a recent discussion I had with a musician friend. When, in 1978, guitarist Eddie Van Halen included the guitar solo entitled *Eruption* on his band Van Halen's first LP—that's a long-playing record, for the benefit of anyone reading this who's under 40—it included a nearly 2-minute-long section with a playing technique previously (almost) unknown. It was so unique that Eddie would turn his back on the audience when he played this section at live performances. The only way other guitarists could access the secrets of this technique—and everybody

---

6   In the three years from 1999 to 2002, the amount of new information produced nearly equalled the amount produced in the entire history of the world previously. (Darling-Hammond, 2010)

wanted to, as it was the most exciting new sound to come out of the instrument in more than a decade—was to find a player who had somehow worked it out or a teacher who could teach it. Both were very rare, and the latter was expensive.

Trained as a child on classical piano, Eddie took up the guitar as a teenager, though he was largely self-taught. For many centuries, players of the guitar and similar instruments had used the left hand to strike the strings and the right to hold the strings against the frets, altering the length of the vibrating string and so altering the resultant pitch. Eddie's piano background told him that both hands could be adding notes to the sound, and he took his right hand to the fretboard, effectively playing separate parts with each hand on the guitar. In the pre-internet age, this technique took many years to spread through the guitar world and it can be heard on hundreds of hit records through the 1980s (most famously on Michael Jackson's hit *Beat It*, where the solo is actually played by Eddie himself). Today, a quick YouTube search for *Eruption* brings a plethora of results including numerous tutorials, children as young as 8 playing it and other tutorials showing and telling how to play it on instruments including the ukulele, piano and bass guitar.

Whether you want to simply change the oil on your car or build a bomb (as the media often remind us) you can find instruction, in easy steps, from a number of different sources on the internet. The same applies to every aspect of playing the guitar, the drums or the kazoo. Even highly specialised information and techniques can be found somewhere on the net. Specialisation is not as special as it once was.

I know of a hardware store employee who, with no training in the area, asks a customer with a tricky question to come back to him in a few minutes, during which time he googles the problem and appears as an instant expert on the customer's return.

Ms Kim Roy was one of eight teachers and principals who in March 2019 provided anecdotes to the Brisbane hearing of the Federal Government's inquiry into on the status of the teaching profession. Her story provides an excellent example of how a teacher's understanding of her students can lead to positive learning outcomes when they have the autonomy to be able to make decisions about learning.

'I was teaching a group of year 9 boys in central Queensland poetry,' Ms Roy told the hearing.

'They were all country kids, rugby league-mad. Trying to teach them poetry felt like knuckle-bashing.

'All the traditional resources, all the structures that were put in place, it was not going anywhere, but the moment I got my hands on some Rupert McCall poems and we could throw in some footy-based poems, all of a sudden it went "boom": they were interested.

'Because it was all about footy. It wasn't about poetry, it was footy. We know these kids in front of us. We know the big picture that we want to try to get them to, but we can tailor that best if we've got that freedom of autonomy.' (Moore, 2019)

One Australian teacher whose career has straddled the introduction of standardised testing and curriculum is Gabbie Stroud. She recalls first encountering the standards movement during her first year of teaching in London in 1999, before it had become a major factor in Australian schools. In *Teacher: One Woman's Struggle To Keep the Heart in Teaching* (Stroud G., 2018), the author writes how her grade 5/6 class was worried about the SATs (Scholastic Aptitude Tests), noting: 'I watched as students became tired and disinterested during lessons where we covered endless dry content and wrote texts that were almost clinically manufactured ... I couldn't buy into the feeling of pressure ... perhaps because I knew, even then, that standardised tests revealed very little about student learning.'

She continues, fondly reflecting on Australia where the GERM hadn't yet spread: 'I was lucky to be returning to a country where I wouldn't have to worry about SATs and performance requirements and shame and standards. In Australia there wouldn't be someone looking over my shoulder, checking I'd done my job, forcing me to prepare students for exams they weren't ready for. I wouldn't face newspapers with threats from politicians and depressing downward graphs. I wouldn't have someone testing my students as a means of testing me.'

But that was all about to change.

'What are our educational objectives? Students who learn a curriculum and regurgitate information become compliant adults and are great for making armies.'

Sanna Lukander, Finnish education writer and creator of the mobile game 'Angry Birds'

— Brett Mason, SBS News, 2018

In many ways, Gabbie Stroud exemplifies the teachers described in the headlines that opened the first chapter of this book. She details the frustration when the standardised marking system was introduced: 'The thing I never liked about A-to-E [grading] was that we never acknowledged effort. Surely the student's effort is of as much value as his or her achievement.' Gabbie never felt comfortable with this 'C is the new A' system (for those not familiar with it, a 'C' on a report now meant the student was working 'at standard' and an 'A' or a 'B' indicated they were working a year or more above 'standard').

'Something inside me wanted to rage against this imposition ... I thought of a younger me flipping herself inside out to achieve an A and hating myself when I didn't get it.' She was told that this new system was more rigorous, more standardised, more professional. Then she describes the silence that followed as everyone at the staff meeting pondered the unspoken and tried to hide their offence at being told that what they were now doing was not rigorous, not up to standard, sub-professional; and resisted the urge to scream, *'How would you know? You never come into my classroom, you've never seen the way I assess.'*

On the introduction of the rubric system that accompanied the new grading regime (designed to describe what each level of achievement looks like for the student), Stroud recalls the first day she returned rubrics to students following what used to be one of their favourite lessons each year, a self-portrait drawing art class: 'Four kids cried. Gordon threw a pencil at his portrait and Jane-Anne said she'd do an even better one at home that she would bring in for me to grade. Narelle's parents have made an appointment to come and see me tomorrow. They're concerned because Narelle only got a C.'

Not all parents strive to see their children achieve high scores on NAPLAN as these comments on a Pasi Sahlberg interview in *The Guardian* demonstrate: 'My daughter has just completed year 1 here in WA and she struggled. She pushed against the constant pressure to fit into the model of a perfect Australian six-year-old and consistently demonstrated that she learned more while working in a hands-on situation (arts, moving around, science experiments and nature trips) as opposed to sitting still, doing worksheets and informal tests. Towards the end of the last term her teacher started telling me that she needs to focus more on her spelling "for the remainder of the school year" because "we'll be testing on that a lot more in year 2". My reaction: well, that's for year 2. After a whole year of being beckoned almost every day because of my daughter's inability to conform and being academically behind (although her semester one AND two reports indicate her being smack bang in the middle—i.e. average) I'd had enough and pretty much told them to back off.

Unless they decide they don't want to be singled out (and I would understand that), my view right now—and my husband's—is that neither of our kids will be taking the NAPLAN tests. I checked, you can withdraw at any time and you don't have to give a reason. Well, I have a reason: don't use my kids to measure teachers' KPIs. Find another way of checking that they're doing their jobs. There are people who say that they need to practise being tested so they are used to it by the time the high-school exams come around. To that, I say my generation weren't tested in primary school and while I wasn't academically gifted and passed very few exams at first attempt, plenty of my peers did. Those 43-year-old doctors, nurses, lawyers, teachers and engineers all around us—they didn't do NAPLAN (or SATs in the UK).'

And another parent: 'One thing that stood out to me in my six-year-old's reports last year was that all the things she's really good at—art, craft, outdoors-based learning—were dismissed, not even commented on. Just a score. A strong message that in this teacher's class, in this school, in this country—these things don't matter, these are not strengths, these are nothing more than hobbies.' (Pasi Sahlberg, 2018)

In summary, 'They're getting hung up now on grades rather than thinking about their learning.' When Stroud says, '... thinking about their learning', she is talking about students being immersed in the activity of drawing a self-portrait, and all of the creative possibilities that this can entail. Unfortunately, I have never seen a rubric that included as one of its criteria 'student enjoyed' or 'was immersed' in the task. Surely a successful arts lesson or course is one where the students continue the practice of painting, drawing or playing, rather than obtain a good grade but after doing so the student never does the activity again. I am reminded once more of Sir Ken Robinson: 'If you run an education system based on standardisation and conformity that suppresses individuality, imagination and creativity, don't be surprised if that is what it does.'

For Stroud, the introduction of NAPLAN came as a final blow. 'This idea that we can compare schools based on test scores, it buys into an idea that parents can shop for schools like they're shopping for insurance. I mean, the tests only cover two subjects. This My School website can't tell you the wellbeing of the students, the experience of the staff, the context of the learning ... Schools are not about this. Schools are not businesses. Schools are schools. You can't put them in a graph. You can't capture them in a test.' (Stroud G. , 2018)

Stroud elaborated on this idea on the ABC's *Q & A* television program: '... it's this blanket, one-size-fits-all, "Let's just churn it out and sprinkle out the education on all these kids and, presumably, they'll all come out the other end and things will all be fine. And we'll collect a whole bunch of data on it and the graphs will go up." And, you know, I'm here to tell you they're not. The graphs are going down. The students are disengaged. The teachers are struggling and something needs to change.' (*Q & A*, 2018)

Stroud's own daughter was in tears at the thought of doing the NAPLAN tests and Stroud herself was struggling to find the sense of meaning that had once driven her teaching. 'We were implementing new spelling programs in an effort to improve NAPLAN results. We were formally testing the students more regularly just to keep them in the habit. We were gathering more evidence than ever to justify the grades on report cards. The word "accountability" dogged my working days. I had lost all sense of autonomy and had learned to stop asking "Why?" I had never been one to play much sport, but I still knew the feeling of defeat.'

On *Q & A*, answering a question from a student named Alyssa, Stroud lamented the standardisation of education: 'Well, I have very serious concerns about NAPLAN and they, again, speak to that idea that I've raised about the standardisation of education. And I'm really actually quite tired of hearing about how NAPLAN is just a snapshot and it's just a couple of days and it's just this and it's just that. Putting the word "just" before these things doesn't absolve NAPLAN of the impact that it's having on our students. So Alyssa's question earlier, or her comments, you know, Alyssa is of the generation now she would have been doing NAPLAN right from year 3 all the way through. And what we're seeing now is (that) our students are disengaged, they're disheartened. You know, they're not excited to come to school. They're not enthused about their learning. And this is the effect that NAPLAN's having.'

On the argument that NAPLAN provides 'valuable data', Stroud was quite pointed: 'Look, it's offensive to me to hear that before NAPLAN we didn't have any data. We did. We have teachers. You go in and you knock ... Thank you. You know, as a teacher I do incredibly important work. I engage with these students and I follow them step by step through this learning. And I can tell you at the end of the day, albeit that I will be exhausted, but I can tell you what that child can read now and what new gains they made with their writing; and where they're up to with their maths. I am human as instrument assessor. And that's important. That is valuable. And all of this, "We'll throw out the NAPLAN test and then we'll get this result", saying that … it's like blaming the X-ray for the bone being broken. The bone's not broken. We have teachers there and they have important skills, they have important understandings about assessment. And we need to value them because we are losing that. And it's a great, great tragedy.' (*Q & A*, 2018)

Finnish academic Dr Mervi Kaukko, now working at Monash University in Melbourne, has said that teachers in Finland are highly respected and have a lot more autonomy, and they would not accept the idea of NAPLAN. 'I think in Finland teachers and principals would find it pretty insulting that someone would come and tell them what they need to do differently to fix a problem that's shown by data collected during one day a year, for example.'

The attitude in Finland is that they often know what's best for their students.
— Dingle, 2019

Gabbie Stroud started seeing a psychologist and wondered if she would ever feel normal again. Her teaching time was consumed by evidence-collecting and creating folders of professional standards, which 'felt like an insult and a threat'.

Lana, a colleague of Stroud's, summed it up: 'I've got thirty years of teaching experience and here I am printing out this excursion note as "evidence" and writing a reflective summary of the excursion to show that I can ... *plan and implement well-structured learning and teaching programs or lesson sequences that engage students and promote learning*' She shook her head. 'You'd nearly laugh at that if you weren't already crying.'[7]

When Stroud saw her doctor about chest pain, he told her, 'It could be a heart attack or it could be your heart is broken.'

This was the end of the career she had craved since she was a child. I strongly recommend *Teacher*, Stroud's book. She pours her heart out describing how she gave everything to the profession and the students she taught, the profession that ultimately almost destroyed her.

'At the end of my teaching career I thought I was burnt out. I thought that's what had happened to me. But I've since done a whole bunch of reading and a whole bunch of research on this, and I realise that I wasn't burnt out, I was suffering the effects of demoralisation. And what demoralisation is, it's different to burnout but it has similar symptoms. Because "burnout" suggests that I didn't manage my resources well enough, that I didn't take care of myself well enough, that I didn't get my assessments done on time, that I should have done a bit more yoga and maybe eaten some more vegetables. Right?'

'Demoralisation is something very, very different. Demoralisation is this idea where you as a professional know very, very clearly what is best for your students and the

---

7   Professor Robyn Ewing from the University of Sydney referred to this problem recently: 'This is our obsession with teacher accountability playing out. ... We've made it an adversarial profession, when it should be collegial. Teachers are competing for positions and constantly trying to make themselves look highly employable. What they should be focused on is their students and their teaching.' (Stroud G. , 2017)

direction you should take them in and you are told again and again to go in another direction. And that is demoralising. I'm sorry, I'm going to get upset now but that is demoralising for me as a professional, for someone who brings herself to the classroom and to the work and to those children every day. So I think we need to start having a very serious think about and conversation about NAPLAN and the impact that it's having and, more broadly, that idea of standardisation.' (*Q & A*, 2018)

In their book *The Global Fourth Way*, Andy Hargreaves and Dennis Shirley found that of the top-performing countries in the world in education, not one tested its children on almost all of the curriculum year after year.

One might also ask, 'If testing is so bad, why are we taking any notice of the PISA test results?' Indeed, many teachers in Finland were unimpressed with their country's rankings in PISA tests for just this reason. They asked, 'Are we doing something wrong that we're making our students so good at tests?'

PISA tests are not like ordinary tests. 'We were not looking for answers to equations or multiple-choice questions. We were looking for the ability to think creatively,' said Andreas Schleicher, who is from the OECD and a key scientist behind PISA. (Ripley, 2013)

In researching her book *The Smartest Kids in the World*, Amanda Ripley sat the PISA tests herself, under the same conditions as the students, and found that PISA was more than just a test of facts. It tested the ability to do something useful with facts. One question in the language section asked students to evaluate the effectiveness of a sample flu-shot flyer.

'Yes or no, the only way to get full credit was to defend your opinion by citing at least one specific feature of the flyer and evaluating it in detail. It wasn't enough to merely repeat that the style was "friendly" or "encouraging", those words were already included in the question … The assessment had to be original and expectations were high …' (Ripley, 2013)

PISA demands fluency in problem-solving and the ability to communicate: in other words, the basic skills I needed to do my job and take care of my family in a world choked with information and subject to sudden economic change.

Echoing the sentiments of Sir Ken Robinson, Ripley asks, 'What did it mean for a country if most of its teenagers did not do well on this test? Not all of our kids had to be engineers or lawyers, but didn't all of them need to know how to *think*?'[8]

---

8   The PISA test measures the ability of 'young people to use their knowledge and skills in a variety of real-life situations, rather than merely on [*sic*] the extent to which they have mastered the school curriculum' (OECD, n.d., p. 6). PISA, therefore, does not use curricula from various countries as testing material: rather, it assesses the students' ability to use the knowledge gained in schools. PISA uses the testing age of fifteen in order to measure 'how far students approaching the end of compulsory education have acquired some of the knowledge and skills essential for full participation in the knowledge society'. PISA has helped redefine educational goals by assessing 'what students can do with what they learn at school and not merely whether they can reproduce what they have learned'. (ibid.)

EDUCATION SPENDING

We need to move beyond the idea that an education is something that is provided for us and toward the idea that an education is something we create for ourselves.

— US educationalist Stephen Downes

Education at a Glance, a study published by the OECD, contains figures that allow international comparisons to be made of educational spending. The countries listed here spent approximately these US-dollar amounts on education per student—from primary school to tertiary academy—in the year 2007:

- United States $12,100
- Norway $10,800
- Denmark $9800
- Sweden $9100
- Iceland $8300
- Japan $8200
- France $7900
- Germany $7800
- Finland $7800
- United Kingdom $7300
- OECD average: $7600 (OECD, 2007, p. 170). (Chung, 2008)

Amanda Ripley concluded that simply spending more on education did not necessarily improve it. 'Everything—everything—depended on what teachers, parents and students did with those investments. As in all large organisations … excellence depended on execution, the hardest thing to get right.'

Ripley answered the question why any country should strive for excellence in education (when there are those who see it as a waste of money, or something required only by a minority) by reminding us that 'Economists have found an almost one-to-one match between PISA scores and a nation's long-term economic growth. Many other things influenced economic growth, of course, but the ability of a workforce to learn, think and adapt was the ultimate stimulus package. If the United States had Finland's PISA scores, GDP would be increasing at the rate of two trillion dollars per year.' (Ripley, 2013)

Data suggests that 'kids at American private schools performed better, but no better than similarly privileged students in public schools'. NAPLAN data from October 2018 revealed this to be true in Australia also, one report stating, 'There is little difference in student progress among Catholic, independent and public schools.' (Natasha Robinson, 2018)

The fact that private schools are still bound by the same standardised testing—and to a lesser degree curriculum— suggests that these may be more important factors in educational outcomes than the better facilities and organisational independence of the private-school sector. (Schleicher, cited in Ripley, 2013)

Now an Australian resident, Pasi Sahlberg—in his new role with the NSW Department of Education and as adviser to the Gonski Institute and Future Schools—noted that while the Government's own Gonski report called for equity in educational funding, the government response was otherwise: '... when I see the schools where there are obviously needs for children to get support and help and different types of programs, those resources, they're often human resources, but often also money is not available: that's something that, in many other countries in the world when I travel around, I see exactly the opposite, that the resources and investments are going to those communities and schools where there are more needs in the children.'

'You know, there are many things I still don't understand in my new country here, and one of them is that these very same people who say that money doesn't make any difference in education, then all of a sudden sign a $4 billion cheque for those schools that actually already have a lot of money and resources. So, you know, if you put Australia into the big picture internationally, one thing that makes this education system, education systems, here very different is the way they are funded.'

Ironically, it is the students least likely to encounter a wide array of educational resources at home who are also least likely to encounter them at school.

'Almost all the other OECD countries are giving more money to those communities and children where there are more needs, except Australia. And that's where you are very different. This is not only my opinion, you can read what the OECD and many others are saying even more loudly than you can hear right now.'[1]

He continued to make his point in a manner that perhaps only an outsider looking in could: '… if I look at the research and statistics about where the additional funding here in Australia has gone, for example, since 2008 most of the additional funding has gone to non-governmental schools. And these schools … only cater for about 15 percent of disadvantaged or Aboriginal children. I think it should be the other way around, that the additional money should go to those schools and communities where there are children who need more to be educated better.' (*Q & A*, 2018)

Indeed, *The Guardian* reported, 'All 24 of the schools … supposed to lose money (following the Gonski report) received a funding increase in 2018 because of bonus funding set up to help private schools cope with the transition to the Gonski 2.0 funding model.' (Michael McGowan, 2018)

A *Guardian* opinion piece by Chris Connor and Bernie Shepherd noted that, 'Between 2009 and 2015 total per student

---

1   In virtually no other developed nation do we see governments so readily throw money at a fee-charging private sector, enabling them to turn public schools—the Government's **own** schools, to which more than 60 percent of Australians send their kids— into low-income ghettos, even as educational inequity threatens the nation's prosperity. (Szego, 2019)

funding to independent schools rose by 34%, to Catholic schools by over 40% and to government schools by just 18%.'

Around the same time as Pasi Sahlberg made the above statements, a Canberra newspaper ran the headline '*Students turn to sugar daddies to pay tuition fees rent*'. According to the report, 'Students are increasingly seeking alternative methods to offset the financial pressures of university, with the average cost of a degree in Australia rising to almost $30,000 this year.' It added that a website had been created to facilitate this 'transaction'.

On the website it says, 'Finding the right Sugar Daddy can help a Sugar Baby stay ahead of the game and get the education they need without the burden of a mountain of student loan debt.'

'… Tuition and enrolment numbers continue to increase, and millions of Australian students are looking for a way to get out from underneath the crushing weight of loan debt.' (Canberra Times, 2018)

In a striking counterpoint a few months previous, the *Helsinki Times* reported on the Finnish debate over the cost to secondary-school students of purchasing textbooks, noting: 'Well over a quarter (29%) of general upper-secondary students and their families struggle to cover the costs of education, found a survey by the Finnish National Agency for Education (OPH).' Finland also funds the education of foreign students in the belief that significant numbers of them stay on to work in the country, thereby giving back the skills and knowledge they have acquired.

'Costs are the reason for many to drop out of upper-secondary education, and this is what many upper-secondary students now want to change,' says Alvar Euro, the chairperson of the Union of Upper Secondary School Students in Finland.

'Concerns have arisen especially for those students who are worse off,' he adds. 'A lack of money should not seal off the education path for anyone. This is an important issue to us, and we hope it is such also to Members of Parliament.' (*Helsinki Times*, 2018)

Indeed, Australia is already one the leading countries in in the world when it comes to education spending, at about 6 percent of gross domestic product. A report by the Organisation for Economic Cooperation and Development released in 2018 found that in Australia 'by 2015 the share of private sources of non-tertiary education made up 19% of overall spending, the most of any advanced economy and double the OECD average of 8%'. This can be rephrased, as one leading international newspaper did: 'The proportion of public money being spent on private schooling in Australia is higher than in any other advanced economy and has increased significantly over the last decade.' (*The Guardian*, 2018)

Tellingly, it added that the OECD had 'found the proportion of public money spent on primary, high school and vocational education decreased significantly between 2005 and 2015'.

> *Director of Regent Consulting Paul O'Shannassy, whose company finds the right private-school fit for students, said about one in 20 families that came to him planned to remortgage their home to pay fees ... 'Many people will pay $700,000-$800,000 from prep to year 12'*
>
> — Sunday Herald Sun, 2019

It's very difficult to argue with Sahlberg's take, given the above figures. Indeed, Australia's system of private schools resembles that of the United Kingdom, which one writer described thus: '(It) underwrites a hierarchical form of social organisation, and philosophy of individual freedom, intrinsic to the (Conservative) party's philosophy.'

> *The Turnbull Government's Gonski 2.0 is a precious opportunity to lock in fairer deals on school funding. It should be seized by all sides of politics. Australia's long and toxic funding wars must end so we can move onto other much-needed education reforms.*
>
> — Sonnemann, 2017

As that comment quoted in *The Guardian* suggests, it has long been obvious that equity in education funding is a huge issue in Australia, yet at the time of writing we have seen no action despite virtual unanimity in public sentiment, as a glance through the comment section following articles such as the above attests.[2]

As in Britain, the system is entrenched in Australia and Melissa Benn's observation of the British system applies here

---

2   A recent story in *The Guardian* described how the writer stayed up late making cakes to sell to help fund a primary school's visiting music teacher: *Recently we hit our target. The principal announced to the children lined up one morning that they would be able to have their music tutor come back and teach them again next year. The kids cheered. A couple of days after our last cake stall, it was reported that Knox Grammar had just opened a $47m new facility, including a performing arts centre housing a 750-seat auditorium, purpose-built dance studio and soundproof rooms for one-on-one musical tuition— no doubt funded in large part by parent and community fundraising, just like my own little school. Although when that school talks about hundreds and thousands it means dollars, not sprinkles. One can't begrudge the children at Knox their professional-quality soundproof recording studio. Nor the Presbyterian Ladies College its orchestra lift, nor [Sydney college] Scots' $29m castle-esque library. It must be a fine experience indeed to learn and grow in those schools.* (Ribeiro, 2019)

also: 'Now, more than ever, there is a strong moral and political argument in support of integration. At a time of growing divides and damaging inequality, we urgently need public institutions that bring the nation together, not [ones that] further separate and divide us. For many in the UK, the idea of a unified education system to which all subscribe is too great a leap of the imagination, too daring a proposition—and yet the benefits of a common schooling could be immense.'(Benn, 2018)

Benn makes an excellent point, one that is common knowledge in Finland where all education is free and private schools are virtually unknown, 'On a more raw political note, the greater the spread of families using a public service, the greater the pressure on politicians to commit sufficient funds to support it. Or as David Kynaston puts it, rather more amusingly: 'One only has to witness pushy private-school parents on the touchline to realise that the state sector will never achieve its full capability without them.'

Australia was quick to embrace the standardisation of its curriculum on a national scale with the introduction of the Australian Curriculum. Inspectors are routinely sent out to all schools to ensure that the Australian Curriculum is being documented (I wouldn't say 'delivered') appropriately in all corners of the country. If it is of such immense importance that all students across the country are indeed studying the same curriculum content, then why is it also not of immense importance that they do so in similar classrooms, in schools with similar facilities, philosophies and resources? An example of this is a primary-school teacher who told me that she was not allowed to use her exceptional musical talents—transforming the alphabet into song—to assist her grade-prep pupils with learning the alphabet and other basics because her colleague in the adjoining room (also teaching grade prep) could not offer this to her class.[3]

Somehow, the fact that some students are being taught in buildings worth millions of dollars with features such as indoor swimming pools while others are in portable classrooms without air-conditioning or heating does not apparently require 'standardising'. When the Australian Curriculum stipulates that all students study physical education until the middle secondary years and inspects the curriculum documents of each to ensure this, surely the fact some do so in a school with multiple sports fields, swimming pools, rowing facilities, tennis courts, indoor basketball courts and links to professional sporting teams, and some with none of the above, means that all students across the country are not receiving the same *standardised* physical education?

Robert Verkaik, writing in the book *Posh Boys*, labels the private school system in England (which is something akin to our Australian system on steroids) an 'apartheid education system'. The promotional material for Verkaik's analysis reveals that something positively scandalous is afoot:

> Imagine a world where leaders are able to pass power directly to their children. These children are plucked from the nurseries and sent to beautiful compounds far away from all the other children. They are provided with all the teachers they need, the best facilities, doctors and food. Every day they are told this is because they are the brightest and most important children in the world.

---

3   See 'Julianne' in the Appendix of that name.

Years later they are presented with the best jobs, the grandest houses and most of the money. Through their networks of friends and family they control the government, the courts, the army, the police and the country's finances. They claim everyone is equal, that each person has a chance to become a leader. But this isn't true.

If such a world existed today wouldn't we say it was unfair, even corrupt?[4]

Nothing moves like the speed of trust.

— Stephen Covey

Pasi Sahlberg has made the following observations on the Australian teacher: 'Maybe the key for Australia is loosening up a little bit, less top-down control and a bit more professional autonomy for teachers,' he says.

'One way to think about it is maybe, you have all these good things—funding, your economy, good teachers—but you're not improving. Maybe the problem is that things are tied up in a system that is not able to be flexible enough for teachers.

'Maybe there is not enough trust in Australia in good teachers.'[5]

---

4   At the time of publication of this text, calls for the scrapping of the UK's private-school system are growing, with support seen from both government and opposition sources, and in many quarters of the media.

5   One Finnish teacher (Saara Tahtela) made the following observation on this point: 'What sounds unbelievable in my Finnish ears is all the talk about "poor-performing teachers". The reason for this, naturally, is because we don't have any tests or standardised evaluation of

But the secret to Finland's success is more than just trust, although that is a key component. As one writer noted in the *Los Angeles Times* recently, 'The lesson of Finland is that success isn't about individual wealth, power or prestige—or even high national GDP or advanced technology. A country is successful when it meets the needs of its citizens and creates the conditions for people and communities to meet their full potential.' (Ollila, 2019)

Any country decides what its educational outcomes will be when it selects, and perseveres with, the government that puts the system into place. The more one looks at countries like Finland in search of the secrets of their success, the more obvious it becomes that educational success is linked to other factors like child poverty and social equity. I believe that Australians want all of these: we just need to allow the conversation to occur. Isn't that what the famous Australian motto of 'a fair go' is all about? Wasn't that the goal when we broke away from the rigid social class systems of old England?

As I rode a bus to the airport at the conclusion of my last visit to Finland, it occurred to me that I had never encountered an angry, upset or even agitated Finn. Even at 6am and with the temperature at zero, the people seemed remarkably upbeat. The driver navigated the early morning traffic easily, stopping to assist every passenger on and off with their baggage. On arrival I was informed that my Norwegian Air flight (the cheaper

---

teachers. It would be very hard for me to even imagine where to start if someone asked me to draft a plan on how to evaluate a teacher's work results. Talking about results in the same sentence with teaching is a little complicated since the results are not always immediately visible or noticeable, but they may come later on in the life of a student.'

option) had been cancelled due to a pilot strike. Within an hour I had been placed on a Finnair flight taking me to my destination earlier than my original flight and at no additional cost. Perhaps the 'Happiest Country' tag should be replaced with 'Most Content Country'.

> *For a long time ... thousands of years, the idea of going to the moon was so impossible that people actually used it as a metaphor for impossibility. And then, in the 1960s, we humans did it. And the take away from that is that anything you set your mind to, you can do. Von Braun said after the lunar landing, 'I've learned to use the word "impossible" with great caution.'*
>
> — Jeff Bezos

A BRIEF (RECENT) HISTORY OF TEACHING IN FINLAND

In early December 2001, Finnish educators received some surprising news: their students had outperformed peers in forty-three other nations—including such powerhouses as the United States, Germany and Japan—on a new international assessment of reading, mathematics and science skills, the PISA test.

Finland, declared an OECD study, produced the world's most literate citizens. What's more, Finnish schools were uniformly good, displaying the narrowest gap between high and low scorers. Many factors have contributed to Finland's academic success, from highly trained teachers to a culture that encourages reading. One key—and exportable—ingredient often gets overlooked, however. Finland's remarkable performance today springs directly from education policies and reforms set in motion four decades ago. Although the process sparked criticism and political debate at its inception, there now is general agreement that the early policy decisions of the 1970s were correct and helped create the celebrated school system of today. (Erkki Aho, May 2006)

The 1960s and 1970s were times of drastic change as Finland evolved from an agrarian society into a Scandinavian welfare state. To facilitate this transformation the education system, which maintained the inequities of the class society for which it was designed, needed a total overhaul. Adopting a 'comprehensive school reform' approach, Finnish educators and policymakers scrutinised everything from curriculum and textbooks to salaries and administration. At the same time, teacher training underwent substantial revision, aimed at raising the standard to university level. (Erkki Aho, May 2006)

In 1978 and 1979, new degree requirements for teacher training in Finland were confirmed. The new university departments of teacher training (replacing the previous teachers' colleges) were responsible for teacher training and research on teacher education, teaching and learning. To standardise and 'academise' teacher training in Finland, it was decided that all comprehensive-school and upper-secondary teachers had to complete a master's degree. The curricula of teacher training programs were unified and based on either the science of education or the subject to be taught. In practice, this meant class teachers majored in the science of education, subject teachers in the relevant field.

Administration of the system was decentralised at the end

of the eighties. The intention behind this was to improve the quality of education by increasing flexibility and introducing new evaluation mechanisms. The statements of education policy in the 1990s reiterated the strong belief in social progress through continuous development of education. The Finnish approach to schooling had been centrally planned, but with emphasis on decentralisation, local decision-making and grassroots responsibility.

In the early nineties, Finland endured a deep economic depression. The education system had to adapt to sharp funding cutbacks. At the same time, the downturn spurred new educational efficiencies and forced decision-makers to seek fiscally sustainable solutions. The education system played a central role in helping the whole society cope with problems of high unemployment. (Erkki Aho, May 2006)

During the 1990s, school-specific freedom in regard to curriculum development expanded based on the principle of regionalism and, later on, responsibility for the development of teaching and curriculum was transferred to school boards. Teachers' work was no longer centrally directed and they were given more and more responsibility for planning and development. The 1994 National Core Curriculum for Basic Education supported this aspiration. It emphasised the responsibility of teachers and schools in curriculum planning and stressed collegial cooperation at the local level.

Education development has been balanced between innovation and sustaining practices of proven worth. The two are not always opposites. There has been public recognition that many necessary innovations already exist somewhere in the system. This was an important acknowledgment of teachers' wisdom and the realisation that learning from past experience is equally important as introducing new and often alien ideas in schools. (Erkki Aho, May 2006)

During the 1980s and 1990s, Finnish teacher training started to embrace the idea of considering teachers' work as constant research. Teacher training, seen in this light, leads on to qualifications for a multiskilled professional, a sort of 'super degree'. Many of those who apply for teacher training have a special talent as their strength. They are students who are musical, artistic or athletic *and* linguistically, mathematically or intellectually gifted; they are students whose success at school has encouraged them to apply for teacher training.

The teacher's task and position are respected: in fact, they are downright honourable. In Finnish society, teachers are considered capable of changing the future and championing ethical and social goals as well as social equality. The teacher's responsibility for, and impact upon, pupils' development are seen as remarkable.

There are eight universities in Finland offering teacher education programs and one offering such a program in Swedish. Each university determines the entry criteria and the number of places on offer. Eight thousand applicants competed for 670 places in primary-school teacher education degrees in a single year earlier this decade (VAKAVA, 2012). The length of teacher education programs in Finland is in general four to six years depending on the speciality chosen. The basic qualification for primary and secondary teachers in Finland is a Master's degree. In Australia twenty-two universities offer teacher education programs, and it normally takes four years to become a primary or secondary teacher, while for graduates with a first degree it is one or two years. (Uusimaki, 2010) Student places in teacher education degrees are uncapped, and the criterion for selection is how well an applicant performed as shown by year 12 results, or through securing a first degree for graduate entry. (Uusimaki, 2013)

In Finland each university offering teacher education programs has a school attached to it. For example, if a university offers a primary-teacher education program then there is a primary school attached to the university. The school's teaching staff are highly qualified professionals who lecture at the university in a variety of subjects and are qualified in mentoring skills.

Dr Tuija Turunen, senior lecturer in primary-school teacher education at the University of Lapland, in northern Finland—and currently working as a post-doctoral research fellow at the Research Institute for Professional Practice, Learning and Education at Australia's Charles Sturt University—has described in detail the selection method for entry into the University of Lapland's Primary Teacher Education Program.

'The first stage in the process of being accepted into teacher education programs is to complete the national entrance examination, which is called 'VAKAVA' [National Entrance Exam for Educational Studies]. It is a big thing and happens at the same time all over Finland. Based on the results of this test each university then selects the students they want to invite to the second stage of the entry process, which commonly involves group and individual interviews.

'At the University of Lapland we provide a Primary School Teacher Education Program and our intake is about sixty to sixty-five students per year. We had approximately 900 applicants seeking entry to our teacher education program in 2010 and, based on the applicants' VAKAVA results, about 240 applicants were invited to the second stage of the selection process.

'At the University of Lapland the second stage involves participating in a group discussion and that is followed by individual interviews. We have several interview panels with three panel members on each of them. The panel consists of a senior lecturer, a primary classroom teacher from the primary school attached to the Faculty of Education and a junior faculty member. During the group discussions the applicants are allocated to groups of four to six (members).

'They are provided with various educational topics to read (up on), and then each applicant is required to lead a ten-minute group discussion. During the group discussions our role as panel members is to observe the participants. We have guidelines to help us to do that. After the group discussion each applicant is interviewed individually for approximately ten minutes about their reasons for wanting to become a teacher.

'… We are looking for leadership qualities where a person is confident and can take charge, but not to the extent that they actually don't listen to anyone else. We are looking for personalities who can be polite and empathetic. We look for someone … able to include those who are not talking or contributing to the conversation.

'So we are looking for people who are able to listen to others, who can encourage others and who have the ability to make others feel included: "Oh, that was a good point, I think" or even "I don't agree with that. Can you explain a bit more?" Things like that—there are always applicants who talk, talk, talk but who are not saying anything important.' (Uusimaki, 2013)

The teacher-training program includes a number of 'practicums', or what in Australia are known as practical placements, involving time in the classroom. The trainee may even complete this in another country. The fourth and last practicum is called the 'advanced practicum'. The focus of this practicum is to support and develop pre-service teachers' sense of 'teacherhood'. This concept refers to reflection on being a teacher. For example, the applicant will examine such questions as, '*What kind of teacher am I? What kind of teacher do I want to be?*' What we want to see and what hopefully happens is that pre-service teachers develop their own understanding and, most important, their own personal pedagogical philosophy about what it is to be a teacher. From this emerges pedagogical knowledge about '*what I am supposed to do*' and an understanding about how to combine theory and practice. (Uusimaki, 2013)

It is common for Finnish teachers to undertake 'projects': they might be doing a joint project with a school in another country, or working on a research project. One teacher I met has taken a group of automotive students to China to exchange ideas with a school there. Government funding is made available for projects that can potentially improve the knowledge base and education of students. This is an extension of the idea that the teacher is also an education researcher, much as a university lecturer in Australia (or elsewhere) is expected to conduct research in their field while also discharging teaching responsibilities.

As explained earlier, education leadership has been gradually distributed from the centre to the local level. Leadership is not limited to daily managerial duties and administration, but also respects the responsibility and right to lead continuous development of the education system. (Erkki Aho, May 2006)

Each school's autonomy is different, depending on which municipality it is situated in. The nation is divided into 311 'municipalities' of various sizes, the smallest being an island where just 500 people live. Its only school has about fifty students. The largest municipality is Helsinki, with 600,000 inhabitants and about 250 schools. In some municipalities schools have the right to hire teachers, while in others teachers are recruited by the Government. In some, principals can approve minor bonuses for teachers; in others, all salary income is provided by the Government. (Sahlberg, https://pasisahlberg.com, 2018)

> In studying foreign systems of education we should not forget that the things outside the schools matter even more than the things inside ... and govern and interpret the things inside.

— Michael Sadler, 1900 (Chung, 2008)

Finnish teachers know they can work independently and as responsible professionals in education—professionals who, thanks to their training, can develop their work and evaluate it from various social and ethical perspectives. (Sitomaniemi-san, 2015)

The purpose of education in Finland is holistic development of the student's personality encompassing knowledge, skills, values, creativity and interpersonal characteristics. Schools have remained places for learning and caring where learning comes before testing and achievement is defined in relation to one's own development and growth rather than universal standards. (Erkki Aho, May 2006)

According to Webb et al. (2004), Finnish policymakers' conception of teacher professionalism is exceptional, with the idea of empowerment at its core. Constructivist theories of learning have led Finland to move away from centrally prescribed national curricula towards school-based curricula with active learning pedagogies, changing teachers' roles and responsibilities. (Webb, 2004)

In 2006 Pasi Sahlberg et al. identified several factors behind the success of the Finnish education system.

1. Comprehensive schools that offer all children the same top-quality publicly financed education—not only excellent teaching but counselling, health, nutrition and special-education services as well—seem to play a key role in building a high-performing education system. Good schooling for all, not for some, is the core value that drives education in Finland. This equity principle has been the leading policy idea since the early 1970s.

2. Education reform in Finland has been evolutionary rather than revolutionary. From very early on, all stakeholders accepted that there could be no quick fixes in building a system to provide good education for all—and that very few short-term changes would be sustainable. Finnish schools have learned to change and changed to learn.

3. Success of the education system is politically, culturally and economically intertwined with other sectors of society. The same factors that promote a well-functioning economy, strong public institutions, the rule of law and a democratic civil society embedded in a dynamic welfare state also support academic achievement. To analyse and understand an education system, one also must examine its political, social, and economic contexts.

4. A stable political environment is crucial. But Finland has succeeded in creating sustainable leadership and

education reforms because policies and principles are based on firm long-term vision, hard work, goodwill, consensus and respect for the professionals whose knowledge and insights yield the best solutions and decisions. (Erkki Aho, May 2006)

Finnish society's belief in equity cannot be underestimated in this discussion; however, as demonstrated by the lack of distinction in Finnish education before the late 20th century, this alone does not create the successful system.

Finnish people are notoriously quiet, almost shy in their manner.[1] Some suggest that this comes from the extreme winters and isolation in parts of the country. One 'joke' I was often told is of a bus where each bench or double seat is occupied by one Finnish person and the driver calls out, 'This bus is full.' As I visited Finnish schools to speak about Australian culture and music to English-language students (usually around year 9), I was continually struck by the silence in the room as they sat waiting for the class to begin. They would sit at the back of the room, much in the way Australian students do, but rather than take advantage of this distance from the teacher to chat among themselves they would sit quietly, and when instructed to move to the front would do so immediately without complaint. I am of the belief that the practice of allowing students regular breaks between classes prompts such a willingness, as the students are

---

1 A recent newspaper report under the headline 'Small talk is cheap: Finland could teach us the art of keeping quiet' made note of this phenomenon: 'In Finland, the concept of idle chit-chat barely exists; Finns report being surprised when total strangers try to engage them in conversation at airports. But as the global economy brings the world to their doorstep some Finns have begun to take lessons, in classrooms or from private tutors.'

aware they will soon have a chance to interact socially, removing the need to try doing so during class time. Undoubtedly, the respect with which Finnish educators are held in society is also a factor, as is the priority given to education.

One Finnish teacher explained the silence thus: 'The silence in the class seems to speak for being shy when you are not familiar with your teacher. When they get to know their teacher, they are more than talkative and have opinions on everything. They are also complaining on different issues, like where do I need this or that knowledge, why do I need to study this subject etc. But this is a common problem at any school, I think. Many students are very easily distracted nowadays and easily bored during a lesson (we teachers will never be able to beat the passion they get from their mobile phones etc.). The schools are well equipped with devices and pupils are demanded to write many projects during a year, yet as a teacher you have to watch over [them to see] that pupils stay on the right websites and don't start to play *Fortnite* or other popular games instead of doing the project.'

A teacher at one of the schools I visited, Clasu in Tampere, called it 'the best school in town', adding that 'the students are highly respectful of teachers', with a hint that this might not be true of all Finnish schools. Their teacher felt that, 'Maybe, rather than just being shy and quiet per se, Finns are slow to warm up. Once they know the people they are talking to they can be extremely talkative.'

Pasi Sahlberg also points out that 'there is a common misunderstanding when discussing Finnish education internationally. People think [the] Finnish education system is unified. However, in fact, education in Finland is very diverse, not the same everywhere. That is also why I often tell international colleagues that we should go out and see different communities in different situations and with different needs in Finland.' (Sahlberg, https://pasisahlberg.com, 2018)

A PERSONAL HISTORY OF FINNISH EDUCATION

The following is a personal account from Oili Turunen (mother of my good friend Mikko), a student and later teacher in Finland through the transformation of the country's education system from unremarkable to one of the best in the world. It should be noted that it was at the end of the nineties that the United States and other countries started to adopt standardisation, and soon afterwards Finland topped the PISA scores and continued with its own system. These interviews have been translated from Finnish, though at times some of the phrasing has been maintained. There was clearly no awareness that she was part of a broadly admired education success story (her story predates the PISA results that made the system famous), although it is clear that a positive student relationship was always central, with teachers accorded both respect and autonomy.

In the 1940s the teacher was an ideal, to be looked up to and to be obeyed. As students, we studied exactly according to given model. Religion and patriotism ruled. We had our own school lunch with us and each had their tablecloth on top of their school desk, made at first school year. My school in the east of Finland was also a war hospital so we went to school in a prayer chapel.

Catechisms had to be learned by heart, I believe we all had to stay after school, when we couldn't. We took lingonberries to school to eat and spent time raising potatoes at the field. The term 'parallel' school system meant that kids had to apply for the middle school (mostly upper class and from the towns—these students had the options of further education—not so much from the countryside). I applied and got in from third grade (when my older cousin did as well). I received a recommendation from my teacher.

During the 1960s the school network was increasing in size and it seemed that new schools were being founded everywhere. People's school versus middle school was still a thing even during the beginning of the decade. Fortunately communal middle schools started to appear in so that even the lower-classed children had a chance to enter academic studies if they had 'a head for studies' as it was called at the time. Middle schools and their teachers, too, had more esteem. So-called citizens' schools that were the route from 'people's schools' to vocational schools had surprisingly lot of variety in subjects.

I taught (I was a teacher now!) bookkeeping, economic geography, sales, mathematics and typing for instance. Class size was roughly thirty to thirty-two pupils. No disciplinary problems were present. The downside of that system was that the people's-school-citizen-school route had fewer opportunities for further studies than the middle-school route.

To prevent smoking at school I would hold a regular bag inspection. When I checked Hannu's bag (he was a nice boy) I told him, 'If I find something here I will faint for sure' for he was not the type to smoke. Hannu (forty-two years old now) reminds me of this even today when we meet and says: 'No need to faint today.'

Basic education arrived in Finland, coming in our small eastern village of Rääkkylä in 1972. Teachers were running from course to course in order to learn this new system. We were allowed as much time as we needed even during a summer break. There were courses on new pedagogy, a new style of mathematics (I had to learn about groups and sub-groups or such nonsense!) and everything else. Very important and interesting experiments were the different-level studies of languages and mathematics: short, medium and long. I thought they were a very good idea. Each level group was given the kind of teaching they needed.

(This is a reference to a form of streaming, which was used for a while.)

The level courses were removed in 1985. Now everyone had to go to every possible continuation studies because supposedly the background was the same. I wonder if that was the reason that we were required to study all kinds of different pedagogical methods? Student-centredness, groupwork and information-searching were among the 'buzzwords' of the day. Sometimes I felt that methods were tried out because of the methods themselves, not because of learning. I learned that it was a good thing to: think for yourself, filter the information, evaluate yourself and what you have learnt. It is not important to pack information to your brain, but rather to know where to find it.

For English class, I recall that I had packed a suitcase full of stuff for a trip I was supposed to make. I can still see my class, whose task it was to go through my luggage and mark in small pieces of paper what I had packed, in English of course.

During the 1990s there was a lessening of government subsidies for schools, and particularly remote areas were suffering. The teacher's influence and autonomy were reduced (not good) and students were suffering. There was internationalisation, and the school's independence on what to teach was in question. The latter not necessary a good thing. How to compare kids coming from different schools? How about if the family moves to a different town?

I have always been a spontaneous teacher and my motto was 'Remain the glow of enthusiasm'. I believe that I have given the students the freedom to think with their own minds.

The history of the teacher's pointer is interesting: at first a sturdy wooden stick that allowed pointing, scaring and punishing. Then a plastic thin thing that was used like a conductor's baton, then a telescope. You never know how far you needed to reach. And now a mouse.

How did the autonomy of the teacher change during these years?

For me there was no change, because I have always tried to be original and independent. The school system has let the teacher be the person she is. This is good when the teacher has talent; on the contrary when teacher is boring and does not care about the job, there is no-one to guide the teacher.

Changes in curricula?

I have never followed curricula too closely. Changes really have not had too much effect on my job.

Status of the teacher?

Again in my case there was not a lot of change. I have always maintained very close and relaxed relations with my pupils. I always had good relationship with their parents as well. I allowed students to disagree with me, even encouraged them for that.

How about public perception on teaching, teachers and education in general?

The teacher used to be more appreciated both by parents and students alike. Nowadays it is not necessarily so and that is very unfortunate. In the 1970s teachers were valued. Students behaved mostly well and even though we were all on first-name basis that had no impact on the teacher's status.

How has funding changed?

Where I was (a small village in east of Finland) I pretty much got all that I asked for. For example I had electric typewriters as soon as I needed them.

When computers came, I also was able to start teaching writing with them.

Nowadays schools seem to have fewer resources; before it was easier.

Facilities, classrooms and tools?

Each class were in their own classroom, we were more connected with one class group. However, different age groups were integrated within some subjects so that a classroom was divided by, say, a bookshelf. Some teachers used pointers, that changed from wooden one (in the fifties and sixties) it was used also for punishing) to plastic. I never used it.

Qualification requirements?

They depended on the subject. For subjects like mathematics and languages, teachers came from universities; for subjects like woodwork and crafts, teachers came from so-called seminars (equal to today's universities of applied sciences). There was a lot inequality within the teaching staff.

Especially before the 1970s reform, those teachers that taught in private schools were in a better position than the rest. After reform all were equal.

Attitude and behaviour of students 1960s versus 1990s

In the 1960s teenagers respected teachers more so than they did in the 1990s. However, students became bolder in expressing their opinions. This had lots to do with individual teachers' motivation. I have always had a great relationship with my students. Teens must be teens and adults, adults.

After the reform some subjects changed, for example set theory was introduced in mathematics. Teachers were trained in new pedagogies during summer breaks.

Groupwork became the norm in the 1980s. Finnish teachers have always been very diligent on accepting new methods. I got my best ideas from short courses (child theatre, choreography). The courses were very useful. I also used lots of motivational methods like giving students opportunities to ask questions and then together searching answers from whichever place, for example by calling the Finnish Parliament. This way students get to experience feelings of success.

Oili retired from teaching in 1996.

EMOTIONS IN THE CLASSROOM

FÁBIO D'AGOSTIN

… in the 2015 PISA Finnish students still reported close to the highest level of life satisfaction out of participating countries, and the lowest level of schoolwork-related anxiety.
— Brett Mason, SBS News, 2018

I've been teaching mathematics, science and physics for three and a half decades. I never considered doing anything other than teaching, and never really had any interest in another vocation. I always found teaching to be demanding yet interesting enough to mean I never really thought of leaving the profession … it's a really rewarding job actually.

As a Melbourne University graduate majoring in physics and mathematics, I spent the first seven years of my career in the Catholic system, working in a couple of girls' schools—one for girls from quite a high socio-economic background. They were good kids: they behaved. I had classes of thirty-seven to thirty-nine students (this was in the early to mid eighties).

Then I moved to a more tech-flavoured school with a vastly different clientele: they were far more 'needy'. The school took some real 'hard nuts', I guess you'd call them. Their experience of school had been pretty disastrous. They hated school, hated teachers. This was the first time I had come face to face with the needs of desperate kids. You could almost fool yourself, in schools with students of lesser needs, that by performing the role of a conventional teacher you were doing fine, that you were meeting the students' needs, but suddenly you found yourself in a furnace-like atmosphere where the students' *affective* needs (the need to be cared for, the need to be loved etc.) were so raw in every classroom you entered ... that's when it dawned on me. There were kids there who couldn't sit still, couldn't concentrate, who cursed and swore at you and hated you just because you were a teacher. To get anywhere with children such as these it became obvious I needed to address other sides of their education. I had to let them know that, no matter who they were, I was interested in them and—more than that—concerned for them. Failures were plentiful, but the successes I did have were marvellous.

Those successes still remain my greatest learning experiences as a teacher. I listened to these young people. I listened when they talked to me and when they spoke to each other. I listened to them out in the yard, I tried to pick up on their interests and on their problems. I thought hard about what I was teaching them and about how I was teaching them. I had to be quite creative in my approach but there were ways through and around the walls between us: there's no manual on how you go about teaching kids with the sorts of issues these girls presented.

My research interest has come straight out of my professional practice. It's not just a recent thing, it stems from observations I've made in the classrooms and schools I've worked in for decades. Now in my fourth decade of teaching, I find that issues, problems and characteristics—of classrooms and students alike—have remained the same throughout that time. Technology changes—culture, too. Human nature doesn't.

Human needs—things concerned with what we are and what it takes to get us to learn—will forever remain at the core of the teaching challenge. So long as our business is teaching human beings there are inescapable things about the demands of that occupation that we do quite poorly, to be honest. Throughout my training and my indoctrination into the profession it's always been about cognitive stuff: it's academic. In maths and science it's about rules and formulas and solution processes. That's what I measure my students on: I teach them, I test them, I rate them. The sum of what I appraise my students to be is all about academic performance and sides to the students apart from this are treated incidentally, as if they don't matter or are getting in the way. What am I talking about? About kids needing to feel important, to feel cared about, to feel involved, about their need to see meaning in what they're doing in the classroom. I don't measure, or directly teach, these things: I never have.

I frequently listen to experts in the field touch upon the affective elements of this. They talk about motivational issues, they talk about giving content meaning, making it something they will find personally beneficial. But, rather than being an incidental suite of needs for our students, I'd say they're central. You've got to be ticking those boxes. What do students want to learn? What are their histories? What are their attitudes? Where are they at when you first get them? What are their interests?

I am a big believer that at the heart of so much of what we desire in our students—interest, motivation, engagement, perseverance and creativity—lies emotional positivity. What are these emotions? Happiness, a sense of involvement, of belonging, comfort ... they're pretty basic needs. I think that to deny these, not to recognise them in our teaching, is a deficit.

Wellbeing as a concept is very important, and I know many schools have programs for this. Until wellbeing infuses our classrooms and is shoulder to shoulder with academic needs, we've got work to do. I'd argue that to achieve the academic results that we hope for, that we *say* we want to achieve; we must have a strong sense of wellbeing as our starting point.

In particular, as a classroom teacher required by society to implement an academic program, I have often felt under-equipped when it comes to addressing students' emotions; connecting academic exploration with those basic emotions. If I can have students feeling happy about what I'm doing, comfortable and enjoying what I'm inviting them to do, I've got a far greater chance of gaining traction with my academic imperatives.

Never give up on kids, no matter who they are and what they are. Never ever disown them, or diss them at all. Keep your eyes and ears, and your heart, open ... they're kids, they're needy ... they need to be cared for. The toughest street-fighting kids, and there were a few of them at the first schools I taught in, would melt when they realised you cared for them regardless ... you cared for them without strings. You weren't there to oppress them, take advantage of them, dismiss or punish them. When that penny dropped ... it was powerful.

My interest in emotions was piqued by these early experiences, and this became the basis of my Ph.D. thesis: *How can I elicit a positive set of emotions? How can my work help my students to enjoy my lessons?*

Starting from the students' vantage point I've made use of emoticons or emojis: kids know them well these days. I asked them to submit emojis throughout the lessons I was teaching them. These were year 10 students who I had been teaching for some six months. I organised lessons to come in phases or sections where they could provide feedback via the emojis. One would be a chalk-and-talk activity from me, one a worksheet activity, another might be an unfamiliar problem with no structure. We had practical activity in there, teacher-led discussion, student-led presentations. I ranged across in many ways typical working styles and pedagogical approaches that I'd always employed, and explored them through the lens of '*How do kids feel about it?*'

I received some interesting responses: some predictable, some not. Many students loved chalk and talk, and that's all they wanted me to do. They were 'maths kids' and I think mathematics is often characterised as a chalk-and-talk-type subject: 'Tell us the formulas, tell us the steps and that's all we want to know.'

That finding was intriguing as it contradicts many of the messages your proponents of 'quality maths education' push because pure instruction is not an optimal way to have students learn. I think that's been established, which for me raises one of the issues of our times in maths education: How do you take students away from that belief that mathematics is learned through rote, that maths is learned by repetition? How do you perhaps not prise students away from that but build on that?

No doubt repetition and rote has its place in maths, such as in tables where in many students it establishes valuable knowledge and understanding. But when these types of pedagogy are all that maths is, then you have a problem.

So how do you get students participating in unconventional activities such as practical problems, exploring open-ended problems where there is no correct answer?

UNCONVENTIONAL 'RICH LESSONS'

Apart from the conventional chalk-and-talk or worksheet-type lessons, I also used a series of unconventional lessons or 'rich lessons' that would be novel in the students' experience. They were open-ended, exploratory, investigative, unfamiliar. One example is the 'Four 4' exercise where a student has to use the digit 4 four times in a row with any mathematical operation (plus, minus, divide, times) between those 4s and in doing so create twenty sums that yield the numbers 1 to 20 in succession. This was a task out of left field in terms of the curriculum. Mathematics experts will tell you it is a superb activity for any students to be doing because it requires skills vastly different to those covered in conventional lessons. It demands creativity, perseverance and imagination; it invites trial and error, fosters thinking out of the square. Maths educators agree that these are invaluable qualities, the sort that truly make the mathematician but that are sadly neglected in conventional lessons.

In another rich task I gave students a rectangular piece of cardboard and asked them to cut the corners out of it to create flaps so that it could be folded up to make a box. The question was, 'What size squares do we need to cut out of the corners to make the biggest box?' We did this task in the science labs. I gave them cards and scissors, sticking tape and measuring cylinders of water so they could measure the volume of the boxes. They spent all lesson trying to work out what the biggest or smallest cuts were and which would give the biggest box. Once again, the challenge is open-ended and learning takes place without instruction. Year 10s found it interesting: the curiosity was there, the endeavour was there. It was counter-intuitive in many ways as naïve students may have thought, 'The smaller the cut size, well, the more card I've got left and the bigger the volume', but it doesn't work that way. When they made bigger cuts they were getting very small boxes so they had to find an optimal solution in between the two extremes. Non-linear thinking is required, and that was magical. Some students performed in ways that I doubt they had ever done before in a maths lesson.

We train students—particularly in maths— to expect notes, to expect work problems and no surprises in any activity or venture: highly structured, tightly directed by teachers. So my experiences in these classes had been that routine lessons generated a lot of positive emotions from the students. They were happy; they did enjoy them. However, some of the rich lessons did elicit more positive emotions. As a matter of fact, that create-the- biggest-box-you-can challenge was the most successful of all ten lessons in the study. They were very happy to be left alone, to have a purpose and to be organising themselves around solving the problem.

One outcome of my research is that accessibility is a critical factor. What is accessibility? It is the property of an activity that allows a student to achieve progress without scaffolding or structure, and that was certainly the case in each of the five rich tasks I set, with one exception. Having to make their own way through a given problem was a strong element in those lessons. The critical difference between rich and conventional lessons is student-centred rather than teacher-centred.

The learning tasks were not formally assessed at the completion of these activities. To measure learning of a conventional academic kind is not too complicated. To answer the question, '*Do they know how to use Pythagoras' formula?*'—a typical curriculum topic—you would give students a test with perhaps ten problems where they need to invoke Pythagoras, award them a score on completion of the test and safely assume that the score represents their academic grasp of Pythagoras.

What a test or other conventional assessment can never measure, and is not designed to measure, are the answers to questions such as the following:

- Does the set task build their confidence in geometry or their self-esteem in being able to do mathematics?
- Does it build their self-esteem in being able to do mathematics?
- Does it add to a positive attitude towards numeracy and mathematics?

Conventional tests answer none of these questions, yet I think they encapsulate some of the most important outcomes that need to be pursued.

Our teaching cultures should, without a doubt, be more sensitive to assessing those sides of student development. I like to think my research has provided a glimpse into what is out there. I collated all of the students' emoticons over the ten lessons. Each student provided thirty to forty of them and I created a class set of segmented column graphs representing the feedback from each student through each of the lessons. This gave me a picture of the levels of positivity and negativity for each student. Probably the most telling revelation from this graph was that the variation between the most positive student and the least positive was immense. Some gave me entirely positive emoticons throughout the entire ten lessons, both conventional and rich. Then I had students at the other end who were barely positive in either type of lesson. They were bored, or angry etc.

Now what that told me was that this class, which was notionally streamed, had been selected on the basis of previous test and examination performance. Generally speaking they were students who, just about always, achieved below the median score. They were what might be labelled 'the strugglers'. A streamed class supposedly consists of students with similar academic needs. But, when I looked at the affective side of it, I found this huge variation. This led me to ask the question— and I confess I don't have an answer to it: *What if we streamed students on the basis of affective responses?* Would that help us to teach more effectively? What would that do for us? Because within this class there was no affective streaming, they were everywhere, and I'd love to run a similar exercise (the same ten lessons to measure emotional response) for the 'upper' streamed groups. On the basis of their emoji signalling, I suspect I might have got a similar result.

Before I commenced the series of lessons I asked them to write a preliminary statement of about 100 words on the

question, 'How do you feel when you are doing mathematics?'
Again, they gave me a variety of statements which pretty much
reflected what I received in the emoticon distribution graphs.
Just about all their statements were showed a strong correlation
between what they had told me initially and the data responses
they provided later.

What that told me was that these responses were not just
a function of my teaching styles and lessons but ingrained or
'trait' responses. These students had well established patterns
of emotional response. If they have an established positive
response—if inclined to say spontaneously, 'I like maths'—
well, that's great. However, it can be quite concerning if it's
an established 'negative' emotional response. For students to
reach the age of sixteen or seventeen with an entrenched view
of maths that is negative, if they find it boring or uninteresting,
if their spontaneous reaction to mention of the subject is 'I'm
confused by it' or 'It makes me angry' is cause for alarm, all
the more so when a number of students respond in such ways.
There is a strong case for investigating exactly what's causing
these types of reactions and attitudes.

Negative reactions are not only to do with a teacher. For a lot
of people, mathematics itself is 'on the nose'. For many students,
their own parents are the main source of negativity. They tell
them, 'I was bad at maths, so don't worry …' There are gender
differences, though I didn't identify any within this study; but if
I had to guess I'd say that girls receive lots of encouragement for
the belief that they don't have to be good at anything involving
numbers and calculation, and that mathematics is not for them.

The most negative person in my study group, one who
responded 'bored' far more than any other, was a girl. Oddly, she
told me she was bored while appearing to be quite engaged in an

activity, so that may have been a 'message thing' rather than an expression of feeling. Emotions are funny things: they're very much under-researched. In their purest form they are adaptive responses; you feel something in response to an event or a situation. You feel angry or scared; flight or fight. But there's a lot more to emotions than that. They can be a deliberate act, and this girl was using her emotions as a statement to indicate 'I'm bored with maths' and 'Maths is boring'. So the exploration of emotions is actually fraught with difficulty. I couldn't just take that student's emoticon as complete proof that the student was feeling that way at the time. Emojis gave me indications, but I also videotaped and interviewed students post-lesson to dig deeper into the meaning of the emoticons they'd given me. In almost all instances, apart from the one I've just mentioned, the emoticon students provided appeared to be a token of their true emotion, although often that emotion was associated with 'trait': the student was bringing that feeling to class regardless of—and without foreknowledge of—the properties of the task that they were to do.

It's a very complex field, emotions, and we need to learn a lot more about how we as teachers impact students. There are keys already, though, that we know can unlock doors for us, making our efforts more effective and much more valuable.

If there is any hint that standardisation and national assessments are blunting our effectiveness in the classroom because we are 'teaching to the test', we cannot dismiss such a risk and must instead confront it. This is my big concern with NAPLAN and I don't know that anyone in authority has honestly explored, let alone resolved, the impact this has on how and what we are teaching and the values we impart … What are we valuing in our classrooms? Is it tests and the ability to do tests?

Does that mean something? I'd love to see NAPLAN include questions such as 'How do you feel about mathematics?' and ask it of years 3, 5, 7 and 9. Then let's drill down further: how about these questions as well? *'What makes you feel good about maths?'* *'What makes you scared about maths?'*

The way would then be clear to uncover the unknown here by asking what had given them that positive or negative attitude to maths. That would be a huge step forward and could lead to some real change.

A week after my interview with Fábio, he sent me the following study as a further example of the ideas he envisages. The study appears in a book by American educationalist Jonathan Ryan Davis. I have tried to condense the essence of it.

The deficit model focuses on what students lack rather than what they possess (Weiner, 2006), which can set up students for failure and create opposition and resistance within the classroom (Gutstein, Lipman, Hernández, & de los Reyes, 1997; Weiner, 2003).

To determine the impact of punitive and exclusionary practices, the American Psychological Association (APA) established a Zero Tolerance Task Force (2008), which found that schools have less satisfactory school climate ratings when they have high rates of school suspension and expulsion. Therefore, it is critical for schools and teachers to focus on how students' cultures and backgrounds are dynamic (Gutiérrez & Rogoff, 2003), and contextual analyses of their backgrounds can help support and celebrate students' differences (Weiner, 2003). This emphasis on school climate rather than punitive and exclusionary practices should result in schools lowering suspension and expulsion rates and lead to positive outcomes for students. As the ... Task Force found, in the most effective positive behavioural management programs in the United States, schools and teachers addressed student disruption [via] 'high levels of student support and community' (p. 858).

Unfortunately, the use of a deficit model in urban schools can also lead to student opposition and resistance. Teachers who use deficit-model thinking tend to focus more on control and order than on academic rigor, resulting in a lack of intellectual engagement which can cause students to act out (Noguera, 2003). Nearly four decades ago, Anyon (1981) pointed out the relationship between teachers' and administrators' perceptions of students and how students perceive themselves. A few years later, Fordham and Ogbu (1986) found that students often act out in opposition to those negative perceptions. Contemporary scholars have found supporting data on negative outcomes for students impacted by deficit thinking; however, their rationale for these outcomes differs from Fordham and Ogbu's conception of oppositional culture which tends to blame the students for their actions. Rather, these scholars found that students often care about school despite negative perceptions of them (Harper & Davis, 2012; Harris, 2006; Mateu-Gelabert & Lune, 2007; Valenzuela, 1999). As Mateu-Gelabert and Lune noted, 'assumption of an oppositional culture still supports the perception that some groups of students, having adopted an ideological opposition to the idea of school, are simply less teachable than others, and for reasons exogenous to the schools' (p. 174).

Conversely, if educators approach all students as having a surplus of skills and talents, academic rigor can exist. Teachers can do this by focusing on the positive contributions each child brings to the learning environment. For educators to shift their ideology from a deficit to an asset-based model, they must change the way they view and perceive their students.

For instance, when Delpit and White-Bradley (2003) taught students of color, they observed how their students had an ability to question issues of power and control and make their voices heard 'for the sake of their own humanity' (p. 288). They did not dwell on any perceived deficits of their students; rather, they valued the contributions students provided in challenging the status quo by creating a classroom grounded in critical thinking. (Davis, 2017)

APPLYING THE FINNISH SYSTEM

After my first visit to Finland, my teaching was never going to be the same. While it could not in many ways have been more different from the system in operation in Australia today, where we are immersed in what Finnish educator Pasi Sahlberg refers to as the Global Education Reform Movement (GERM), there are elements of the Finnish system—ideas and attitudes—that I wanted to apply in my classroom immediately. I felt as though I had spent time in the future and could now see the iceberg coming, but it is impossible to tell anyone on board the ship (which all aboard believe is unsinkable) that we need to change course as we are not going to find success on this route.

While we are aware that the standardised system or GERM is not improving our results (and that's what we judge everything on), it is the only system we know. Indeed, few are even aware we are in this system, let alone that there is any other. So, like most schools, we double down on standardisation when we feel results haven't been ideal. We hold more meetings and reorganise systems for recording and storing curriculum documents, assignments and rubrics etc. in the belief that ensuring 'everyone is on the same page' will provide better outcomes ... but for whom is not always clear. This is never discussed, neither is the reason or thinking behind how any of this standardisation, or doubling down on it, is actually supposed to bring about the coveted improvement.

Further from this, there is no discussion of what 'improvement' will look like. Does it mean:

- Just 'grades' to be improved? If so, then why? What are we measuring and why do we choose to measure it? Who has told us that our students need more grades?
- The number of students choosing to study a subject?
- Student satisfaction? (Okay, I've never heard that mentioned—but it should be!)

I am reminded of a statement by Linda Darling-Hammond: 'At least 70% of US jobs [and I have no reason to see things would be any different in Australia] now require specialised knowledge and skills, compared to only 5% at the dawn of the last century, when our current system of education was established.' (Darling-Hammond, 2010)

It is for this reason that I attempt to allow students to pursue elements of a particular subject that interest them. Their specialist knowledge and ability to gain and apply it will be their key to the future, much more so than any basic skills.

The major difficulty with applying elements of the Finnish

system in an Australian school is that it goes against many of the main tenets of a standardised education system. One can expect resistance at every turn ... well, perhaps not quite every turn, as we shall soon see.

Some colleagues respond with great interest when they hear of the Finnish system, particularly those working in the arts areas as they are often most aware that their students and subject areas have not been served well by the standards obsession. Conversely, mathematics, science and English have been strangled by standardisation with any suggestion of something contrary to the standardised curriculum quickly shot down due to its non-compliance with NAPLAN, the VCE or whatever the current vector of the standardisation germ happens to be.

Others responded with scepticism. 'Yes, but the Finnish are no longer topping those world scores,' said one. 'But they pay a ridiculous amount of tax to do that,' another added with no evidence, or simply, 'Yeah, but that'd never work here.'

One teacher even suggested that the lack of immigrants in Finland was the reason for their educational success! Of course, none of these observations are true, but people sometimes believe what they want to believe.

I also realise that many of today's teachers were not teaching before the standards movement hit, and know no other way of operating. Indeed, they may genuinely believe that the current methodology is 'best practice'. As teachers in a non-government school in Australia, with students whose parents are supportive of the school environment and the methods currently employed, they may believe that this is as good as it gets.

But is it as good as it could be?

Meanwhile, back at school we find ways to represent every aspect of each student's learning as a number: what has been dubbed the Data Wall. This is a series of bar graphs where students are labelled as 'Below Standard', 'At Standard' and 'Above Standard'. Upon first hearing of this, I suppressed—the modern teacher has to get used to a lot of 'suppressing': asking questions is discouraged—the desire to ask about the tests that gave us this data; the urge to point out that some students were up to twelve months older or younger (going by date of birth) than their peers (which prompts the query: if they were placed a year above or below where they are, how would that change the judgments made on their results?) and that some students are known to take a little longer to absorb some concepts, but because they are far more patient their learning is ongoing and they could be well ahead of their peers as time goes on ...

And, of course, where is the Data Wall for art, music and all the other subjects? I often tell of the Google executive who said that in any pile of job résumés he always looked for the musician, explaining, 'You haven't become a good violin player unless you've got resilience and creativity.'

As a parent myself, it is difficult not to feel a sense of injustice at your child possibly being labelled 'slow' on a 'data wall' in some staff office. I am reminded that every student in Finland starts school at seven years of age and yet within just a few years most of them are ahead of international averages.

Next time I bump into you I may run a quick test on something such as creativity (of course you will have no say in this), compile the results and display them on a data wall. I'm sure you'd be comfortable with this, although what you think about it does not come into it.

In comparing how we got to this place I often resort to the

analogy of a frog in boiling water. The standardised curriculum and testing have been implemented gradually, often as a 'trial program', with teachers (and principals) usually expected to play their role without question. Within a few years we had a national curriculum, NAPLAN, and a belief that all classes must be learning the same curriculum material—the same way.

Anything less than complete standardisation is unacceptable and 'best practice' involves ensuring that everyone is on 'the same page' and no-one is doing anything different! Essentially, the goal is to reduce all learning down to the material on the tests and assessment tasks and avoid *wasted time* on anything else.

Many schools, both primary and secondary, are now introducing computer programs known as 'Learning Management Systems' (LMSs) which I refer to as the 'altar of standardisation'. These systems are an online repository where the entire standardised curriculum can be uploaded, with lessons, resources, rubrics and assignment tasks stored and shared easily. These programs are costly and it is made clear to teachers—who in most cases get no say in selecting these— that they are expected to use them. Many LMS platforms are custom-made for the distribution, collection and grading of assignments. Left unsaid in all this is that the assignments are, of course, identical for every student. The rubric is the same for all—and there is no excuse for anything else other than this from a teacher as all assessments are easily accessed via the LMS.

The LMS has become the conveyor belt of this education system. The material submitted by students cannot be handwritten, despite research in this area telling us that handwriting significantly increases memory and understanding

(Horvath, 2019).[1] If increased understanding isn't a core objective of any education system, what's the point of learning at all? And what does it say that we continue to require that students handwrite standardised tests and VCE examinations?

The conveyor belt was critical to the success of the assembly line during the Industrial Revolution. It was important that every participant did exactly the same thing in exactly the same way, to exactly the same standard. But that was more than a century ago.

So the Australian teacher finds himself or herself bound to the LMS, and therefore bound to the GERM or standardised system. Any resistance can be viewed as Luddite and unprofessional, and therein lies the answer to the Finnish teachers who asked me why we continued to use NAPLAN and other standardised ideology when there was no evidence of their actually improving student outcomes in any way. The LMS also makes the curriculum visible to parents, the implication being that they can expect their son or daughter to be learning the particular set curriculum specified for that particular date. So, in a perverse way, parents are conscripted into supporting a system for which there is little or no evidence that it improves the educational experience.

And what becomes of the teacher? All autonomy, creativity and professional judgment have been replaced by a computerised system of curriculum dispersal, retrieval and assessment that treats every student (and teacher) with inflexible uniformity.

The National Education Policy Centre in the United States recently reviewed a number of personalised learning programs

---

1   Horvath also looks at research into online and e-books versus hard-copy textbooks and the results are significantly in favour of the latter format.

of this type. Its report concludes that they reflect:

[…] a hyper-rational approach to curriculum and pedagogy that limits students' agency, narrows what they can learn in school, and limits schools' ability to respond effectively to a diverse student body. (Reid, 2019)

There are usually ulterior motives for the design and extensive promotion of these systems. As Professor Allen Reid, Professor Emeritus of Education at the University of South Australia, points out, they have 'been a financial bonanza for private technology companies such as Summit [Learning], owned by Facebook founder Mark Zuckerberg. These companies have developed online tests and learning resources capable of tracking the progress of, and devising programs for, individual students.

With such programs, students become automatons moving through standardised progression levels. Creativity and critical thinking are stifled as students are steered down an already determined path. And teachers are increasingly excluded from the process, as planning and decision-making are done by algorithms. (Reid, 2019)

Prof. Reid's conclusion sits nicely with all the goals of Finnish education:

The version of personalised learning Australia promotes should be one that nurtures a love and passion for learning, not one that reduces it to a checklist.

PARENT ENGAGEMENT

From the beginning of the year I decide to see if I can successfully apply some of the strategies, techniques and ideas behind the Finnish system in the framework of an Australian non-government school, amid the testing-obsessed standards system, while keeping clear of the LMS conveyor belt. *Perhaps the change will come from the teachers in the classroom and move up through the system?* This is possibly the only remaining area where the Australian teacher still has some autonomy, although the increasing dominance of the LMS suggests that this, too, may be disappearing. As time passes I find it more and more difficult *not* to want to apply what I learned in Finland and have since confirmed through my reading. *That's what being a professional educator is.*

An introductory evening with parents at the school provides an opportunity to explain some of what I hope to implement. They listen intently, happy to hear their children's interests and passions discussed in the same sentences as their education. The idea that education is about a lot more than achieving impressive grades proves very popular, as does the premise that a student being happy at school and enjoying their learning is of greater importance than said grades. The students themselves are pleasantly surprised to find a teacher who wants to give them choices and find ways to make their learning as enjoyable as possible. I find it extraordinary that they should find this extraordinary.

This 'chat' with the parents is extremely important as one of the key elements in the Finnish system's success is the unwavering belief of parents in the idea that education is about the student, and the teacher is on the same side as the student; striving after a great education for them rather than impressive grades. If the parents don't have this belief, the students are unlikely to. Having explained some of my experiences in

Finland and the associated educational philosophies, I ask questions like, 'Do you want to see your son/daughter getting impressive grades or do you want to see them discovering their passions and enjoying their education?'

There wasn't a single parent who said, 'I couldn't care less about my child's passions. Just get the marks they need to get them into the best universities.'

I am sure there are parents who hold this belief—I am having this discussion with year 8 parents and it might be different with year 10s. But this night I've found that the great majority of parents want to see their children discovering their passions and enjoying whatever activities they choose to pursue in their lives. Once parents and students understand that the teacher, parent and student are all on 'the same page'— discovering what they are passionate about and developing their education around this—everyone is on an entirely new learning plane.

American teacher Timothy Walker taught in his homeland before moving to Finland (he married a Finn) and found it a culture shock to transition from a system that prioritised maximum hours and grades—a system he said nearly destroyed him—to one where in the first few days of the school year teachers played games with students and strove to ensure they were as happy as possible at school before commencing any formal lessons.

At first, Walker saw the Finnish idea of taking a fifteen-minute break for every forty-five minutes of instruction as unproductive use of classroom time. His Finnish students told him exactly how they felt when he pushed them past the usual break time. 'I think I'm going to explode! I'm not used to this schedule!' a fifth grader with a newly formed red rash on his forehead told him on his third day of classes.[2]

Before long Walker changed his methods to those of his peers and incorporated the breaks. 'I no longer saw feet-dragging, zombie-like kids in my classroom,' he wrote. 'Throughout the school year, my Finnish students would, without fail, enter the classroom with a bounce in their steps after a fifteen-minute break. And most of all, they were more focused during lessons.' (Walker, 2017)

I explained this idea to my year 8 students, although it was something I could only apply during double periods (a 100-minute English class!), and then only for five to ten minutes. I was wary that the other classes were not getting this same break and it would only take complaints from a few students in those classes missing out to have other teachers attempting to right this inequity. A by-product of this practice was a form of unwritten (and unspoken) contract whereby students understood that their concentration and application before and after the break would be recognised and rewarded.

---

2   To test this theory, researchers took two groups and taught them a specific skill. After the first group mastered the skill, they took a half-hour break and learnt something new. Next day, the group was tested. They 'tanked' the test but tested well on the task they'd learnt last. The second group learnt the same skill as the first group and took the same half-hour break, but instead of moving on to the next task they went back and relearnt the first skill for the same amount of time. When that was done, they moved onto the new task. They went home, came back, and aced the first and second tasks. Brains are flexible—they are adept at learning new tasks. What this research suggests is that if you stop training a skill right after you've acquired it the brain stays in its ready-to-learn state. If you then train on a second similar task while your brain is still in this plastic state, it overwrites the first skill. It becomes as though you hadn't studied the first skill at all.

Business writer and journalist Tony Schwartz wrote about a similar technique he called 'sprints' in which adult employees were encouraged to work intensely for an hour and a half and then take a break of twenty minutes to half an hour. He states that the usefulness of this practice is based on the body's 'basic rest-activity cycle'. (Schwartz, 2011)[3]

I also take time to explain to students that marks are not the only reason they are at school, despite the fact that the system as it stands does send this message. Many of them are up to twelve months older than others in the class and, while some may take a little longer to absorb new knowledge, this doesn't mean that at some point in the future they will not achieve mastery in this area. The example I give them is that of two year 8 students, one of whom may seem more advanced than the other at this point. If both go on to become lawyers or builders, the one judged 'slower' now may turn out to be a far more skilled lawyer (or builder) by the time both are in their thirties, owing to a passion for law (or building) and continuing to learn about it as an adult, when the other fails to do so. I have seen NSW maths teacher Eddie Woo explain this idea (and I use his illustration in my explanation to my students) when he asks, 'How old is an eighth-grade piano player?' The answer is, of course that they may be anywhere from five to 105 when they sit their grade 8 piano examination. It is understood that people start to learn piano at any age; and progress to eighth

---

3   In his book, Schwartz writes: 'While working on *The Last Supper*, Leonardo da Vinci regularly took off from painting for several hours at a time and seemed to be daydreaming aimlessly. Urged by his patron, the prior of Santa Maria delle Grazie, to work more continuously, da Vinci is reported to have replied, immodestly but accurately, "The greatest geniuses accomplish more when they work less."'

grade when their proficiency increases to the appropriate level: there is no set or even expected time for this.

I make it clear to students that marks are just numbers at the end of a unit of work and only measure a small segment of what is actually learned. Timothy Walker believes that marks actually 'distract students from the joy of learning purely for learning'. [4] Every Australian teacher has heard students ask, 'Will this be marked?' as they decide what priority to give a particular activity or task. Gabbie Stroud also frequently commented on the way that rubrics and the obsession with marks impinged on her students' ability to simply enjoy learning for the sake of it.

WHAT A FINN-LIKE SYSTEM WON'T DO

Adopting some practices, ideas and techniques from Finland will not be a magic bullet that removes all problems in Australia's education system. For instance, teachers in Finland still deal with discipline issues. These are reduced somewhat due to greater student engagement and teacher flexibility—and the greater respect for teachers is also a large influence here—but issues remain.

A recent report on schools in Helsinki described the disciplinary situation: 'In class children are listened to and respected, school lunches are free, detentions are rare and exclusions pretty much unheard of. (School principal Petteri) Kuusimäki gave his last detention fifteen years ago, and is visibly horrified at the idea of excluding a child from school.

---

4   Gabbie Stroud described this in her book *Teacher and I* paraphrased in the opening chapter of this publication.

'As a principal, you can't think like that. We are responsible for these children and their lives. We can't give up.' (Weale, 2019)

Finnish society has undergone many changes in just a few decades. The country's former agrarian-based economy has become an economy renowned for highly specialised services and technology. This has meant many young people are now in roles vastly different to those their parents had, and it is likely this change may explain recently reported differences between the results of boys and girls (the latter do significantly better as many boys have only experienced males doing manual labour among their role models).

Another teacher, Pia, told me of the struggles with technology in schools, a common story everywhere:

> At my school in Espoo [just west of Helsinki] pupils are allowed to use their mobile phones while having their free lunch. This is a sad development. Many of them continue playing, watching films, and they forget to eat or socialise with their friends. Their world seems to be in the phone and you can easily hide yourself in that world. The same thing with breaks. As a teacher you see lots of hanging necks, pairs of eyes watching a YouTube video—no socialisation with friends.

As I tried to integrate some of the Finnish ideas into my own teaching, it was important to remind myself that in isolation they can have only limited effect. At every level the impact of introducing a single idea will be incremental, but the combined result will be a significant improvement overall, and this is reflected in the PISA results. It is difficult for one teacher in an Australian school to change a student's attitude to a subject when a decade of schooling and three or four NAPLAN tests have shaped their mindset.[5]

An Australian teacher who does not adhere strictly to the standardised program risks being labelled a non-team player (this has a very negative connotation) and I have been on the receiving end of a number of dirty looks when I have expressed doubt about the dumb conformity expected of us. As Finnish educators pointed out to me, it is my responsibility as a teacher to look after my students. In the case of NAPLAN, the company preparing its tests is making many millions of dollars so it certainly won't be acknowledging any potential negative consequences. State education departments are obliged to follow suit, and principals risk being shamed if they are seen to prevent students from doing the NAPLAN tests.

So who is looking out for the interests of the child? When he or she brings home poor results, we know who will be blamed.

---

5   A beginning teacher learns from modelling the good examples of a more experienced teacher. Similarly, a doctor may learn new techniques from a colleague. Learning from another's example provides an excellent pathway towards improvement. On a larger scale, fields such as engineering, medicine, and technology often learn from each other and borrow new models. This helps improve the field as a whole. However, when considering an interdisciplinary subject such as education, the lines become blurred. Comparativists from Sadler to Phillips urge those seeking policy borrowing to take into account the context of an education system. As Sadler states, 'a national system of education is a living thing' (Higginson, 1979, p. 49). Therefore, direct borrowing and lending of features becomes problematic. (Chung, 2008)

LEARNING POSITIVE

I began to see different *learnings* as fitting into one of three categories listed below. By 'learnings' I'm referring to topics, subjects or other sections of subject matter being studied at school. This is a matter rarely, if ever, discussed in Australian schools today. The Australian Curriculum is set; there is some dissection and rebuilding to put it into bite-sized units of work for study and assessment; and all classes and students within a school are expected to study and complete that assessment at the same time, in the same manner.

Learning Positive: The student has a genuine interest in doing this and wishes to learn about whatever it may be.

Learning Neutral: The student has little feeling either negative or positive: more likely than not, this applies to topics they may not have studied before.

Learning Negative: The student has a dislike of, or 'negative interest' in, the topic, sees no reason for learning it and would avoid it altogether if given the chance. As Fábio D'Agostin's research suggests, this usually stems from a negative interpretation of previous exposure to the topic (often, alas, via NAPLAN).

Educational neuroscientist Dr Jared Cooney Horvath has an explanation for what I call Learning Negative. At some point the student has personalised their lack of success in this area. 'When we interpret [an error] as a threat to our personal identity, not only do we typically ignore that error but we also avoid situations that could trigger the same error in the future.' (Horvath, 2019)

A student's test results can be predicted according to where their various *learnings* fit according to this scale. Conversely, students' chances of learning anything will depend on how they see the subject matter on this scale. Fábio D'Agostin's research paper also supports this idea. The Finnish system also fits in nicely with this idea as students and teachers are encouraged to follow their interests and passions.

Allowing students to have input into their learning—just like giving teachers the autonomy to let this happen—creates ownership and engagement with the learning matter.

A student in one of my year 8 English classes, Ben (not his real name), had been diagnosed with ADHD and had difficulty with English. In the first lesson, Ben was quick to inform me of his lack of ability or enthusiasm for the subject; however, we both connected on the fact that he loves fishing and each week I would compare notes with him on where they were biting and the details behind their capture.

'Catch anything this week, Mr Lawrence?' was Ben's standard greeting before launching into a minute description of the events leading to his fishing exploits' success or failure that weekend. His understanding of tides, fish behaviour and the techniques involved in their capture showed an impressive depth of thinking.

Most of Ben's written English work is rushed; it lacks any proofreading or attention to detail. I have no doubt though that, were I in a position to assign Ben the task of writing a paper on the details of how to catch a fish in Port Phillip Bay, or wherever he had been casting a line recently (rather than Shakespeare or whatever novel the class had been set), I would witness a great improvement in the standard of his writing. Obtaining positive feedback for this task (to which he has applied himself with more enthusiasm than on any English task he's ever done!), Ben will soon be viewing his relationship to English, teachers of English and school as a whole in a more positive light.

Imagine if this type of thinking had been Ben's experience for all of his eight or nine years of schooling. He has been reading and writing about things that he is interested in and his teachers have been giving him positive feedback on all of these. He has not had to sit any standardised tests loaded with material in which he has no interest and which is designed to tell him how far behind his classmates he really is.

From my point of view as a teacher, it is of little consequence that Ben's writing was on the topic of 'how to catch a fish' rather than the themes of a novel set to be studied by every year 8 student. Indeed, the improvement in Ben's self-belief and attitude to English (I hate to use that word 'attitude', it has such a negative connotation) may lead to an improvement in *all* areas of his English. In Ben's case perhaps it is not too audacious to claim that his English has gone from Learning Negative to Learning Neutral or even Learning Positive.

One might argue Ben 'has to learn about recognising the themes in a novel ...' But, while Ben was Learning Negative about English, he was unlikely to learn anything of any complexity and, indeed, pushing him further with rules, or threatening him with poor grades, lunchtime detentions and so on while he was in this state of mind would most likely only have solidified his belief that English was not for him and he was 'no good at it'. Learning Double Negative?

STUDYING HISTORY FINNISH-STYLE
(OR LEARNING POSITIVE)

Identifying aspects of the Finnish education system that can be applied in Australia is difficult, as is identifying the key elements in the system's success. One of these is surely that teachers are encouraged to find alternatives to existing 'commonsense' approaches and every teacher is trained, and expected, to become an innovator themselves. To put it succinctly, teacher training is a huge source of pride in Finland. It is notoriously difficult to gain entrance to university to study education (there are no non-university teachers' colleges) and teacher education is the subject of numerous dissertations. To quote a research paper on the subject of teacher training in Finland:

... the teacher is positioned as a central agent in the aspirations for progress and change. This taken-for-granted idea of the teacher as change agent works from the assumption that teachers, as individuals as well as a collective, are key actors in improving schools and thus in improving society. The definitions of 'improvement' vary in different contexts and times, and may concern one or several aspects related to, for example, efficiency, effectiveness, social inclusion, or wellbeing. Regardless of such variation, educational reform rhetoric most often suggests that teachers—as for example, inquirers, problem-solvers, critical and reflective thinkers, or lifelong learners—will bring about change if they are trained, equipped and instructed in the right ways.' (Sitomaniemi-san, 2015)

Teachers in countries such as Japan and China will often pose a single well-chosen problem to students, contextualised in a real-world situation (as exemplified by Fábio D'Agostin in the preceding chapter) on which they will spend the entire lesson reasoning together. Students will individually and collectively develop and present potential solutions for class discussion and further evaluation until everyone understands the concept from multiple perspectives. (Darling-Hammond, 2010)

A history class I spent time in while visiting Finland was like no other I have seen. As the students worked in silence, immersed in their various projects, I asked their teacher which historical era they were studying.

His answer was completely unexpected: 'We are studying from the beginning of time until the present. Whatever the students choose,' he told me while setting up his materials on the projector for the day's class.

'That is a huge time period ...,' I observed quizzically.

That didn't faze him in the least: 'For many in the class, this will be the last time they study any history, so we want to give them the opportunity to have a very positive experience with it.'[6]

This response, like so much that I found in Finnish education, was ridiculously obvious, so much so that I still wonder why I had never encountered it before. In Australia, too, we are well aware that by year 9 or 10 most of *our* students will never again take history as a subject in an educational institution, yet our curriculum is rigidly structured as if that were a matter of no concern. If indeed a 'fixed' curriculum is

---

6   At the time of writing the trending topic in Finland is 'phenomenon-focused' learning where topics are studied from different angles instead of each subject focusing only on its own slice, this being designed to reflect the way things occur in the 'real world' outside of the classroom. This is quite demanding to the subject teachers but also rewarding as they collaborate across different fields, e.g. geography, English and biology, together.

necessary,[7] then surely some thought should go into ensuring that events such as World War II and the Holocaust are on it. Unfortunately, this is not the case and in most secondary schools a great many students, amounting to a whole generation, complete their schooling without ever encountering these events—and this when the very same right-wing extremism that led to the Holocaust is again raising its head, accompanied again by the Nazi swastika.

'High-school' classes in Finnish history (years 10–12 in the non-vocational sector) cover the subject in a way Australian students would not recognise. Rather than dividing history into eras such as the Roman Empire, Middle Ages etc., as happens in Australia (and in the Finnish comprehensive system—below our year 10), the subject is broken down into themes: cultural, political and social history. Teachers are welcome to offer specialist units of study if they have a particular interest area and providing student numbers are sufficient the unit will go ahead. Each unit usually runs for about eight weeks and may consist of three hour-and-a-quarter sessions per week. In a typical Finnish high school (years 10 to 12) around 20 percent of the students choose to study history at any given time.

Australian teachers have become accustomed in the last few decades to being told what to teach and, often, how to teach it. Assessments are also compulsory, meaning that teachers are obliged to use the same tests and assessment tasks with their classes as do other teachers in the school. This phenomenon

---

7   Trying to explain to students the reason for (and encourage some enthusiasm for) learning about Japan in the 1700s while excluding the twentieth century period (where so many events happened in Japanese history of great consequence to the rest of the world) is a difficult task.

is in direct response to standardisation of the curriculum and standardised tests such as NAPLAN and VCE exams produced outside of the school. The Finnish system, with all its merits, cannot simply be offered to Australian teachers like a new curriculum package.

CONSTRUCTING A FINNISH-STYLE HISTORY UNIT

In year 8 humanities the Australian Curriculum tells us that we will study the Middle Ages. This is a very broad topic, and I have devised an example of how a Finnish approach can be used to make it a Learning Positive activity when, if most students were asked beforehand, it would probably be Learning Neutral at best. This method can be applied to most history topics.

- Firstly, all students watch a 15-to-20-minute 'overview' video on the Middle Ages, which touches on many of the major events of this time including the Black Death, the feudal system and so on. A number of these can be found on YouTube and most schools have videos of this type.

- Before the viewing I ask students to write three or four 'juicy' questions about things in the video they find interesting. A 'juicy' question is a complex question with a 'how' or 'why' element to it requiring some detail to explain it fully.

- Following the video I ask around the room for at least one 'juicy' question from each student—there is often a lot of overlap here—and I write them all on the board.

- Once I have ten or so of these questions I ask for a show of hands from students who would like to work in groups to investigate a particular question and report back to the class on their findings. Students are immediately in Learning Positive mode because *they* have selected the topics to be studied, and the topic they themselves are investigating is one they have an interest in. A year 8 student with no interest in medieval farming methods may find the gruesomeness of the Black Death fascinating (or 'lit', to borrow a term students sometimes use that certainly wasn't used in that sense in the Middle Ages).

- The presentations students give the class are of a noticeably better standard than they would be if students had been randomly allocated topics as they have some enthusiasm for the topic they are presenting and, of course, the student audience are watching classmates speak on a topic they are enthusiastic about.

- Presentations can be varied: I encourage students to include a minute or two of appropriate footage sourced from YouTube or a similar platform and they can include quiz questions, audience participation activities, graphs, timelines etc. Tim Walker also suggests a 'gallery'-style approach where the presenters treat the room (or it could be another space) like an art gallery and have diverse visual material on the different walls and walk the 'audience' through it much like a curator at an art gallery, explaining each 'exhibit' as they go. This has the added benefit of getting the audience out of their seats, a method shown to improve learning in itself. There is evidence to support this 'gallery'-style presentation, with studies showing that memory is strongly associated with special awareness and place,[8] so a change from the usual routine of learning in the same room or seat can stimulate learning. (Horvath, 2019)

- Horvath also points out that the brain cannot process both the written and spoken word at the same time[9], so teacher presentations are strengthened by using pictures (he suggests a maximum of seven words per slide) rather than text projected behind the speaker. Copies of important parts of the text can be distributed after the speaker has finished, providing a second source for the material while boosting memory and learning in much the same way as coming back to it after a break does in the Finnish classroom.

- In a similar way, a set novel can be broken down into various characters, themes and ideas. This is easier to do if the novel has a variety of character types and themes, all of which you would expect to find in a quality novel selected for study in an English course.

---

8   Horvath also spoke of experiments where underwater divers were given information at a depth of six metres. When asked to recall this information, those who did this on the dry land were 35 percent worse than those who did so back in the underwater setting. This has ramifications for teachers who ask students to absorb enormous amounts of information in the same classroom setting. It also explains 'home ground advantage' for sports teams and no doubt affects students doing examinations in different environments.

9   Brain scans show that when we are 'silently' reading, the speech parts of the brain are active, creating a further 'blockage' to the chance of listening at the same time as reading. (Horvath, 2019)

Of course there are always those students who simply don't read. In the Finnish system the methods teachers have used since the child first started school have ensured a sense of ownership and responsibility for their own learning, so there are few 'slow readers', and of course, there is ample access to learning support to assist any students who need it. (The number of Finnish students who access 'learning support' is far greater than here; access is easy, efficient and effective) and in Finland, you won't be surprised to know, there is no 'set text'. Why does there need to be?

Is there something in these texts that every student in year 8 *needs* to know?

If this is the case, then why do we change the set text every three years or so?

Or is it simply convenient for teachers and educators to teach, assess and grade—and then rank students by entering them in a niche on the Data Wall?

If 'management' lacks confidence in the teaching staff, then regimented curriculum becomes a way of managing them, with the assumption that if they are 'keeping up' with everybody else then all must be well.

The missing part of this picture is the student, who has effectively become the 'meat in the sandwich' in a game of teacher (and school) control. Surely, if this type of regimentation is required to manage a teacher who cannot be trusted to work autonomously, then they should not be teaching in Australian schools.

There is a lot more to the success of Finnish schools than just giving students choices about curriculum, but even doing that is not easy within the constraints of our standardised curriculum and testing regimes.

LEARNING POSITIVE: SPELLING

Spelling has always been an aspect of English I place a priority on. But how can I make it Learning Positive?

- A sheet of lined paper is passed around the classroom and students are asked to write their name and suggest a spelling word (or words) that they sometimes have to guess the spelling of. It is okay to misspell the word: this isn't the test. Some students use it as a chance to write some of the most difficult-to-spell words they can think of, but that adds to the enjoyment of the challenge.

- Using the students' completed list I select appropriate words—and sometimes add a couple related to a text we are studying, or common errors I've found in work from this particular class—and we have a collection of words (I do twelve a week) that the students have chosen so they fully understand why they are learning them in the upcoming spelling test.

- The twelve words are written on the whiteboard along with various activities for the students (no more than three or four) such as:

  1. Look up the dictionary meaning;
  2. Write the word in a two-line sentence;
  3. Deconstructing the wanted word which is 'hidden' in front of them by jumbling (or mixing up) its constituent letters (see the grid of letters below);
  4. List the words in alphabetical order;
  5. Find smaller words within the word i.e. breakdown—break, down, own, do;

6. Find antonyms and/or synonyms;

7. Use the words to create a crossword puzzle with appropriate clues (there are numerous programs online to assist with this or you can give out a blank crossword sheet);

8. A crossword puzzle or 'wordfind' you've devised for the students, including all the spelling words plus some others you would like to see them become familiar with—I take these from past or future spelling tests. I have subscribed to website that puts these puzzles together quickly with my words and clues.

The idea behind all these activities (and many more that serve the same purpose) is to make words something students can have fun with and enjoy. Another big plus to this type of spelling activity is that as the students have contributed the words themselves, there is something of a sense that this is 'the spelling test they are giving themselves' as opposed to something imposed on them by the teacher.

B   K   N
A   E   O
D   W   R

The grid you see above could be used in Activity 3. One of the words (containing nine letters) is jumbled in a pattern as I've done here with 'BREAKDOWN' and students are asked to find as many words of three or more letters as they can, however all words must include the central letter (in this case E). This activity is commonly encountered on the puzzles page in many newspapers and students quickly work out strategies to help solve the problem, such as placing the words they have found into columns for three-, four-, five- and six-letter words etc.

At the beginning of next week's lesson there is the 'test'. Again I place little importance on the results as I am well aware that if I can turn working with words into an enjoyable experience, learning to spell will happen as part of the process.

In my experience activities such as these lead to some interesting outcomes. Some of my students who were self-confessed 'bad spellers' found that they were actually enjoying the word activities—I know because they actually told me this. In some cases their spelling results continued to be poor, but as long as I didn't place any stress on this as a teacher (and I think this is a key point),[10] they continued to enjoy the activity and their results did show some improvement. Oddly enough, by the time this improvement happened many were completing the crosswords or other activities for the enjoyment of it and paid little attention to the improved result!

If you think adventure is dangerous, try routine: it is lethal.

— Paulo Coelho

As Horvath would observe, by not making the 'marks' the focus of the entire activity we avoid the 'personalisation' response to the activity known as spelling. We were not triggering any previous aversions here, nor were we creating any new ones. By

---

10 This reminds me of when I used to teach writing to third graders. Only the first few errors on a student's writing would be circled or underlined. What child wants their writing returned with red error markings all over it? As a teacher you are not obliged to *'leave no turn unstoned'* when correcting student work. The content of the writing is always more important than the mechanics, even though both are taught.

avoiding the—for some at least—stressful situation of a formal high-stakes spelling test which can lead to impaired memory and learning,[11] we have created an optimal learning situation with just enough stress to maintain attention and allow growth and enjoyment. This type of spelling lesson, as with much of the Finnish philosophy, has some scientific foundation.

'Frequent short bursts of moderate stress can boost memory and lead to sustained learning improvements. This means if you mix and match the structure, format, activities, discussions and stories you employ … you will make it difficult for them (students) to form simple predictions and [will] ensure they must actively engage with every moment … you can maintain a moderate level of stress and enhance their ability (and willingness) to remember new information.' (Horvath, 2019)

The specific science behind this is that moderate stress can lead to a steady flow of a 'signalling protein', FGF2, which prompts the growth of new neurons in the hippocampus. This is why we hear experts suggest we take up a musical instrument or learn a new language. Continually jumping into novel, unpredictable situations will increase the chances of keeping your mind flexible and memories active. (Horvath, 2019) As

---

11 Educational neuroscientist Dr Jared Cooney Horvath explains how long periods of stress impact learning. Cortisol, the stress hormone that kills neurons in the hippocampus, has free rein to damage our gateway to memory. This withers our ability to access previously formed long-term memories, and makes it difficult to learn new information. Horvath gives the example of being trapped somewhere with no possibility for escape (a possible scenario for us in primitive times). In this situation it makes a lot more sense to block out as much of the negativity as possible and simply survive until the ordeal is over. This is what the long-term stress response does: it helps prevent memories from forming during helpless situations.

long as you quickly move on when the activity brings excess anxiety or pressure, the positive results will continue.

I also believe that beginning school at the age of seven rather than five greatly reduces the chance of the early days at school becoming a stressful experience. The Finnish seven-year-old is likelier ready for school, likelier happy to be reaching this next step of their lives. They enter school with a positive attitude, lowering the risk of stress reaction and of telling themselves 'School is not for me'. Primary teachers enjoy specialist support (e.g. special-education teachers, psychologists and the school leadership team) in deciding what kind of support a student might require. This is also discussed and agreed with the parents.

The spelling test moved from a teacher-centred activity to one that had a genuine purpose and meaning for students, and the most difficult words were understood to be 'challenges' from their classmates, attempts to trip each other up and part of a fun contest. If I haven't passed the sheet around for a few weeks (with three English classes, each class need suggest words only every third week), students often ask when they will get the next opportunity to do so. They also respond to the fact that they now have some control over the activity, some 'ownership'. The question '*Why do we have to learn these words?*' is removed, and participation and engagement levels are much improved.

Towards the end of the year, when I announced to the class that we had done our last spelling test, most students still wanted to do another crossword or wordfind anyway. The enjoyment of playing with words was catching on. It was no longer 'work' but an activity of choice. More than any grades achieved by the class during the year, this was what success looked like.

We don't think about the things we remember; we remember the things we think about.

— Dr Jared Cooney Horvat

I like to think that I will encounter these students on the train or in a café sometime, somewhere in the future, and they may just have a pen in hand and be completing the crossword in the newspaper, or perhaps an online word puzzle. I also wonder how different their experience of school could have been if they had been taught since their first day in a manner that values learning and enjoyment of learning.

Once again, for anyone wanting to find something of the 'Finnish formula' for educational success, a couple of points recur:

- There is no one standard technique or version of any educational practice in Finland. Teachers are asked to study the best practice, then work to find something better;
- If you are trying new ideas and being innovative, you *are* doing it;
- If the only student benefit is 'better marks', you've left the Finnish path;
- If everyone is doing things one way, try and come up with a better way!
- Does it increase student options and encourage creative input?
- Always allow students a break after an hour. Finnish teachers had no idea breaks, one of the few standards they swear by, aren't standard elsewhere.

'Any time you do anything new, there will be critics. There will be two kinds of critics: sincere critics and people who have a vested interest in the old way, who have ... a financial interest to be critics.'

— Jeff Bezos

JULIANNE

Julianne (not her real name) immediately strikes me as almost the perfect primary-school teacher. You get a feel for teachers after working in education for a while. She plays a number of musical instruments, loves working with children and exudes a caring, helpful manner. She has wanted to be a teacher since she was a child, when she played 'teacher' in games with her younger siblings.

The first time I meet her, at a café not far from a quiet coastal hamlet—let's call it Potts Bay—where she started her teaching career, she had not been in a classroom for many months, but was contemplating a re-entry of sorts: trying her hand at emergency teaching. There is so much to her story that I have to arrange a follow-up interview to ensure all is correct and accurate. Originally, I had intended to include more teacher stories: however, Julianne's covers so many aspects that further accounts would likely find us going over much of the same ground.

Julianne's story provides a wonderful insight into the complexities of the role a primary teacher plays in and outside of the classroom.

At our second meeting, a few months later, she has successfully returned to the classroom via emergency teaching and is coming to terms with the extraordinary events which brought an abrupt halt to the career she had long dreamed of.

As we talk, the emotion in her voice is obvious (as is the occasional tear in her eyes). At times she is very animated and speaks quickly, while at other times she slows as a sadness overcomes her, those events triggering memories of the sleepless nights that followed them and the impact they had on all aspects of her life. She avoids coffee, as she has been avoiding alcohol for the last couple of months (she is expecting her first child later in the year). Our final meeting is held almost a year after the events occurred, and unlike my impression from our previous 'chat', my feeling as I leave this time is that she has at last put behind her the events described below.

Julianne is enthusiastic about the reports she has heard from countries like Finland, and hopes that implementing some of these ideas will reduce the pressures on teachers like herself in future.

For the sake of accuracy, I have maintained much of the conversational style.

I always wanted to be a teacher, though at one stage I thought about being a hairdresser, but never seriously. I've got younger siblings and I was always playing 'teachers' with them since I was a little kid. I'd be the teacher and we had this old doll's house and it had all these windows and shelves, and I would put the schoolwork in there that they had to do and so on. I used to teach my sisters and their friends, I'd model my piano teacher and teach what I'd learnt to them. I just love that moment when they 'get' something and being a part of that learning process. Some of the other teachers really just love children and I really do, too …

Working with five-year-olds, every day they were learning something new, even if it was just a letter.

I worked really hard in high school … I don't think I was the smartest kid but I just worked really hard and got good marks. So I went to uni and found it really hard, but I really lived for the teaching rounds. I did a bit of music teaching while I was still at uni and when I first finished. I taught guitar to absolute beginners and I loved that, starting with the basics, it was awesome … just that learning thing again. I'd be bringing in different instruments, and within a few weeks kids learned that Wednesday was music day and they were bringing in things from home, dad's old guitar or drums and stuff, and putting together little bands in the yard. They weren't all great but they were having a go. It was just amazing.

I took a break from uni, working as a careers counsellor at TAFE, before returning, teaching music part-time at a nearby primary school while I studied. I was thirty years old by the time I graduated.

Then when I got my full-time job it was the learning that kept me going. It'd be okay if you had a tough class and all that, and at the end of the day someone went, 'How are you going?', rather than, 'Are your kids at level 7 with this?', or 'How do you know they've learnt …? How do you know they've improved on this? Did you write it down, did you record it somewhere?'

You couldn't just announce and celebrate the learning. It had to be quantified and recorded somewhere.

I can remember in my first year I always kept a bright bubbly mood in front of the kids, but at the end of the day or lunchtime they'd go out (of the room) and I'd shut the door and I cried. I'd sit down at my desk and just have a cry, just because I was so exhausted, just stuffed. Then I'd have yard duty and I'd clean myself up and you'd be back 'on'. I remember one day a grade 6 girl had come into the room to help sharpen pencils and I forgot she was in there and she caught me crying at my desk. She said, 'Are you okay?' … I'd just forgotten she was there!

Physically, my room was removed from the rest of the school, a building on its own. Everyone else would have a team or buddy teacher and in my first three years I was just on my own, in a building on its own. It was really like, 'You're over there, shut the door, and if we don't hear from you it's good.' If you had a new dentist in a dentist building, you wouldn't take the new graduate and put her in the building on its own up the back with some of the patients with the worst teeth and leave her to her own devices, would you? It just wouldn't happen that way in other professions.

When I was the only teacher in that year level it was fine, I could teach in the style I liked. But the next year, when I was teaching the alphabet to five-year-olds, I had a ukulele and I had flashcards that I had made that had the letters with all the kids' names and so on, and so we'd sing it every day and the kids really loved it. Or we'd sing the alphabet with the sounds of the letters … but the girl (teacher) next door wasn't doing that, so I wasn't allowed to do it anymore because we had to do it the same way.

I said, 'This is the way I've learned, and it works for my kids', and so I couldn't do it anymore. But she wasn't able to do it and we had to teach it the same way so that both classes got the same experience. I would secretly do it … it was frustrating, because when I do apply for teaching jobs, because I do play musical instruments, that might get me an interview over someone else who might not. So not being able to use that skill to help students learn is just frustrating. So then we used to try and get the two classes together so that I could do it, but then it had to be more organised, it had to be done at 9.15, but then it was so organised that we lost the joy of it. It was just frustrating.

I had to teach maths in the morning as there were some resources that had to be swapped around, but, in some schools now it must be reading at 9, or maths at 10 … you haven't got that flexibility that if you're going really well in writing you should be able to go for an extra half hour if you need to, because you're the only teacher who's got that class that morning.

I had a boy in my class who it turns out had dyslexia, though at the time he was too young to be tested for it but he had a lot of the symptoms of dyslexia … his mum was really onto it. She was great. We put some things in place to really help him, and we found that just the visual ways of learning things … using photos or connecting words with other kids in the class really worked well with him. So he's gone from learning five words and couldn't learn anything else in the year. The following year he repeated prep and we used this process again and increased his words by seventy and so on. I thought, 'Wow, this is really working for him, I'm going to try this with more kids.' It worked. It was just really enhancing those kids that were already getting it, now they got it faster again. But then when we had the team teaching meeting we had to both do it the same way, and I said, 'But I've got a boy with dyslexia', but 'No, it has to be the same way' was the response.

That should just be differentiation; but it has to be that you're differentiating the same way that I am. It was said that I should not be teaching in that style because the other teacher next door was not doing it that way. Instead of just being able to use my professional judgment, I had to prove that my students were doing better with this method. I had to give a spreadsheet and provide information … I had to *prove* it to be able to do it at all.

I remember the last day of my first year there, the last day of school: you're supposed to take everything down off your classroom walls and so on. The principal said, 'I'm so glad you've taken everything down, your class used to overwhelm me with all of the colour and everything that was around.' I said, 'Oh, I wish you would have told me that earlier, I'm really disappointed to only find that out now.' So the following year I did some research of my own on calm colours, because she blamed the colour of my classroom for making my students hyperactive when it turns out it was actually their different spectrum disorders as they behaved the same in other classrooms but anyway, I used really light browns and lots of colours like that, which sounds really dull but we just went for a real natural look. She told me not to hang work up and not to have anything low and distracting. So I said 'Fine.'

Then about six weeks into the term she came into my room and said, 'I'm so disappointed there's no work up from the students.' I said, 'Look, I'm trying to do this as we said, you see. There's the work above their bags … you told me it was all hanging in front of them and distracting them and making them hyperactive …'

She said, 'No, I never said that. I wouldn't say something like that. You must be thinking of someone else.'

There were lots and lots of little things like this … I know that seems really small, but when there's lots of them, one after the other, it just gets really hard.

I had a five-year-old who had dropped his lunchbox and he just said, 'Well, f***ing hell!'

I said, 'Hey, can you think of another word?'

And he went, 'Jesus Christ!'

I said, 'What about "Whoops-a-daisy!"?' which is what many five-year-olds would say. He looked at me as if to say, 'Are you kidding?'

If you meet his dad, well, he is constantly swearing himself so it was really hard to say anything. When I did, his father said, 'Well, what the f***'s he saying?'

One day the son said to me, 'Oh, Mum hasn't signed the diary. She's a lazy slut!' He's a five-year-old! Clearly he's heard dad say it. I went to the principal and said, 'Look, I'm feeling a bit uneasy about this father. He swears a lot, he swears in front of the other children in the classroom, and he's aggressive too.' The child also had a few learning difficulties, so we had a meeting with the dad, the speech therapist, the psychologist and the principal.

After the meeting I told the principal that I felt quite uncomfortable, a bit uneasy around this man (the father). The principal said, 'He was fantastic … we need to get him to come in and do a talk to the other parents about being a great parent.'

I said, 'I've actually told you that I'm uncomfortable being left alone with him, and I've told my colleagues to ensure that they don't leave me alone in a room with him.' He'd get quite aggressive when he'd speak to me but, instead of supporting me in that, the principal wanted to get him in to talk to other parents! I said, 'You can't get him in to talk to other parents.'

I've always got along well with all my parents, even though some were very individual in their own way, but they still had good hearts … but there's a difference between that and creepy.

Another teacher had a student in her class, his name was Nathan, who had a physical handicap and he had a teacher aide who worked with him a lot, so they had a lot of one-on -one time together and developed a lot of trust. So one day they were talking about something and he said, 'Oh, I've got a sister too.'

She said, 'Oh, do you? I never knew that.'

Nathan said, 'Yeah, we just keep her locked up in the shed, tied up there. We go in and play with her sometimes but … we don't really see her much.'

Nathan is nine years old, so we went and spoke to leadership and said, 'Look, we need to do something, whether this is true or not. If it's not … What nine-year-old comes up with that sort of stuff?'

Nothing was done and school camp was coming up and Nathan's father was invited to join the camp as a helper, even though the teachers were all uncomfortable with this family and we felt that something was just not right. If that's not true, and I sincerely hope it's not, what nine-year-old *is* coming up with that sort of stuff? He would say things like, 'Dad's really happy with you guys at this school, but if he wasn't he says he's got a gun and he would come up to the school and shoot everyone if they don't look after me.'

What do you do with that? And you get told, 'Don't worry

about it: he's just got a very active imagination.' Since then nothing has happened with that family but that teacher has left and I've left.

Another boy, Adam, had a few learning issues. To give an idea of what he could understand, I had a child vomit in the classroom one day, so I sent a student to the office to get some help and someone came with a bucket of sand which they just tip over the top of the vomit and then class continues as if nothing ever happened. So Adam, who had watched all this occur, sees the sand and thinks, *Great, I'll have a play in this sandpit* and proceeds to do just that while I'm trying to explain to him what has just happened. He couldn't understand that because he couldn't see the vomit.

When we had Adam tested, his results didn't warrant a teacher aide.

I had three students with spectrum disorders who shared an aide. In my room I had a boy who had two hours' funding (for a teacher aide), another who had three hours and a third little boy who also had two hours' funding a day. But that didn't equate to three aides, it just meant one aide all day. They just added it all together and gave them one aide, when those boys needed their own aide … it just would have made such a difference. So they were the ones that were funded, but I had two others who also really needed it. At that point, the boy playing in the 'sandpit' (Adam) is the one she needs to be with whereas the other one is actually doing his maths, but she has to leave him because Adam needs her at that point in time. The student who she was supposed to be working with at any time of the day was not getting what they needed because there were these others in the class who took her attention. She always had to stop one of them from playing in the vomit, or chewing on the legs of the table or climbing up the cupboard.

So I made some inquiries and I was given another aide, but for the two hours that she was there they took away the original teacher aide to work in another class! So the department had given me the extra aide, but the school admin took away my original aide.

Getting back to Adam, as soon as I'd say 'Pack your bags' to the class, which we do maybe five or ten minutes before the end of the day, he would think, *Pack your bag', home time, I'm out of here* and you'd look up and he was gone. Someone (usually the teacher aide) would have to go to look for him in the playground or wherever he was. His running away like this was becoming a real problem. So I spoke to his parents about this. They would get to the school at about three (o'clock) and the bell would go at quarter past. He'd see them out the window and that would also make him want to leave early. So I suggested that they not come until quarter past, or perhaps try to stand out of the line of sight of the window, but it kept occurring.

A week after this, Adam's mother came to me—and this gives you some idea of their parenting skills—and said, 'Look, I've got a great idea, I'm going to get a friend of mine to come and kidnap Adam from the school, so he can learn that you can't just run away.' To my great horror, she continued, 'I'll get someone he doesn't recognise to get him and scare him so that he realises that you can't just run away, and if you do you could get kidnapped and he'll never see mummy again and he'll understand not to leave.'

The implication was that he would be sufficiently scared or hurt to ensure he never ran away from a comfortable situation again. I said, 'This is not what I want you to do. I just want to let him know that we want him to be part of our classroom until the very end of the school day. He's not going to understand what's happened (in the kidnapping) anyway … and what about the other parents waiting to pick up their kids? They're going to see this happen and they're going to attack him (the 'kidnapper') or ring the police.'

Mum said, 'No, no … I'll see how it goes.'

I was in shock. She was a nice lady and life was tough for her, but she just couldn't work out a better strategy with her son. I went to the wellbeing officer and I told her what was being planned, and she said we could end up on the news with headlines like 'PREP TEACHER DIDN'T KNOW WHAT SHE WAS DOING' and so on. I told her I was scared and she said, 'Julianne, go to the principal and let her know. This could be very serious.'

The principal just laughed and said, 'Just put it on the student file that that's going to happen.'

I said, 'Pardon? I think we need to tell the social workers that this is going to happen. They need support, this family.'

She said, 'Just put it on the system. It'll be fine.'

So I wrote, 'Told my principal about the planned student kidnapping, she told me to put it on the student system. I suggested ringing the social worker for support.' I just thought, *I've got to cover myself.*

Then, soon after, another boy, Robert—the one who vomited in the story about Adam—started to display some unusual behaviours. He was wetting his pants a lot, playing with his faeces when he was at the toilet, and losing weight: all signs of something going wrong in his life. So I asked the social worker to have a chat to his mother, and she informed me that there had been sexual abuse earlier in Robert's life, and she said that she and another social worker had been to the family home and the father (who was wearing just a dressing gown) had locked them and the mother in the house and would not say where the keys were. She said that she thought they were going to be killed. They had to call the police. This is the father that my principal had wanted to invite into the school to talk to other parents about being a good parent!

He was one of those dads that would just hang around a bit too long in the morning and made everyone feel uncomfortable. When I told my principal about this, and about the social workers' story, she just said, 'I think we're all getting in a tizz and this isn't any of our business.'

I went home and told my husband that I don't even feel safe anymore at school.

The following week we had a meeting at school about mandatory reporting and they clearly told us that, while we had to report anything that didn't seem appropriate, we always had to make sure that we went to the principal first, and 'You never go above our head'. I realised this was targeted at me, and how I had spoken to the social workers (who now refused to visit that family) about Robert's situation.

The next thing on the agenda at the meeting was, 'What goes on the student file?' I got told I had too many incidents on my student files, and I replied that if you look at my class I have a lot of things going on in there. From separated parents to families who are homeless and living in a caravan park and can't pay their bill so they're being evicted from the caravan. If it's something small and I don't think it could affect their learning, then I don't bother to put it on, but I think most of these things could be important at some point.

One father was a builder, he fell off the roof and was going through the stages of recovery from this. The child was four when it happened, going into prep, and he could not tell me a shape, an alphabet letter or a number. He'd just missed all that, all his time had been put to looking after dad in hospital.

Another little boy's parents were separated: mum returned to Indonesia and never came back. Another little girl, her mum's new boyfriend—they were going to get married—he took off to Queensland with half the money for the house that they were saving for. This is affecting the learning of these children, and the kids knew all about it (the problems of the parents). Another's mum is in jail ... she's a great kid but she's in foster care now because her dad's in jail now also. These are all in the one class!

During one class we were learning about shapes and kids were going around the room finding things that were circle shapes, and then we asked them to tell us about things at home that are circles. One says, 'You know those things that are like a glass and you light it ... and there's fire underneath and you put it to your mouth?' The aide and I were looking at each other and saying, 'Yep, we know what they are ...' but we didn't want to name it. (The pupil had been referring to a bong.)

Another dad who was raising a little girl on his own wanted to see me with a few questions, one of which was 'How do you braid hair?' He could do a ponytail for her and he just wanted to be a good father, and you realise that this family are just trying to get by one day at a time.

With another family, mum had a broken arm and she brought a brush with hairspray and some hair ties and said, 'Can you do Chantelle's hair? My boyfriend threw me into a bath and broke my arm in two places and I can't do Chantelle's hair anymore. Can you help me?'

I said, 'I hope he's not still your boyfriend anymore?' and she said, 'We're gonna try and work it out but we're having some time apart.'

So I did her daughter's hair every morning for about four weeks until the arm had healed. I was quite concerned about Chantelle because she has seen her mother get thrown into a bath and quite badly injured, but the office staff told me that if they both seemed to be okay then don't worry about it.

The principal would say to me, 'You need to get used to this, Julianne, just put your big-girl knickers on and toughen up a bit and get used to it.' After she'd said that to me numerous times over the first couple of years I was there, I said to her, 'I don't want to get used to this, I don't want to not get stressed when a mum's been bashed last night or when a boy swears his head off and has no other language.'

The final straw for me was when in one term I had twelve changes to the integration aide that I had in my classroom. There were some bullying issues with the admin, the office staff and the integration aides, some of which are now going to go to the courts, I believe. Meanwhile, I had had to explain all the details about each of the four students who needed support in the class to twelve different people. There was a meeting about the aides (well, that's what it was supposed to be about) and the principal said to me, 'I heard you said this about me, and you were seen crying in the staffroom the other day and made people feel uncomfortable ...'

I responded, 'Hang on a minute, I didn't cry ...' (It turns out it was another girl, Cassie, who was crying in the staffroom.) So

I said, 'I'm sorry but even if it was me, instead of approaching me and asking me what the problem is or am I okay, you're telling me off for crying? I'm sorry, but what principal wouldn't come and see their teacher and say, "Are you okay? Is there anything I can do?"'

There was a teacher crying at the school at least once a week.

Since I have left the school, the girl who took my position has just had a meeting with the principal (who herself had a term off on stress leave earlier this year—then the assistant principal also took a term of stress leave) to tell her that she needs some support with the children.

In my first graduate year of teaching I had twenty-seven preps on my own—seven with special needs including ADHD, anxiety, echolalia, autism, Asperger's and oppositional defiance. In other years I had children—again five-year-olds—from family violence, mums with broken arms due to boyfriends, dyslexia, post-traumatic stress syndrome, auditory processing disorders, a girl with an overwhelming fear of microwaves, parents who could write but not read.

I had no aides during these years—although I filled out all the paperwork and collected weekly documentation about patterns in behaviour for these children, but funding didn't kick in until the following school year.

In my fourth year at Potts Bay I was given 'ongoing' status, meaning that my job was no longer on a year-to-year contract basis. My class size was twenty, I had one aide shared between four students with special needs.

I went through my class list last night and made notes about each child ... remembering this is not a special-needs school ... although the needs of those in this class were overwhelming!

My class of preps from last year. This is absolutely true, although the names have been changed:

Robert has a past history of sexual abuse from a grandparent. His parents decided to double the dose of his ADHD medication without obtaining medical advice. Chronic swearing ('slut', 'c***', 'f***' etc.), social workers refuse to visit the house due to feeling unsafe themselves there. Robert was eighteen months behind in his learning, he had two hours per day funding for an aide. Both of his parents were unemployed.

George's mum has anxiety problems and is a former heroine addict. George suffered separation anxiety and OCD and he writes his own name continuously, uses seven tissues to blow his nose, insists on eating the same lunch every day (otherwise he will have a huge meltdown). Dress-up days were a nightmare for him and his Asperger's was diagnosed late in the year. Funded for an aide two hours per day. Both parents were unemployed.

Johnny has a germ phobia to the extent that he washes his hands after touching any of his classmates. Cries consistently throughout the day. Johnny's parents are going through a divorce and his germ phobia stopped when his parents reunited.

Sam sleeps with his mother every night. His parents are divorced. His mum suffers anxiety, while Sam suffers from separation anxiety.

Cane wears a nappy or pull-ups to school as he has toileting issues. His learning is twelve months behind. His mother suffered severe facial burns while working on a motorcycle while smoking a cigarette. Both parents are unemployed. Cane had no letter recognition after six months and he works with a speech therapist.

Charlie's mother was killed in a car accident when she was just three. She now lives with a stepmother and her father. She is the fourth of five sisters and three half brothers. Charlie sees a speech therapist and she is repeating grade prep. Both her parents are unemployed.

Leigh was born in Asia and his father moved to Australia after his wife left. He remarried to a second Asian wife, who moved back to her country of birth six months later, leaving Leigh and his father alone again. He is repeating grade prep.

Mary's mother is in jail, she has a half sister who is six months old and is in foster home. Mary's dad was evicted from rental housing and is now living in caravan park. (P.S. Dad now also in jail—car theft—Mary now in different foster home.) Mary is a good twelve months behind academically and is repeating grade prep.

Adam has a low IQ, equivalent to that of a three-year-old. He qualifies for special-needs school, says only singular words, played in classmate's vomit when he thought it was a sandpit, would run away from class, parents suggested a fake kidnapping to 'help him understand'. Adam has Coke or cordial in his water-bottle every day. He is funded for aide support two hours a day but the aide is shared with four other students.

Henry is very overweight and always hungry. He's a slow learner with auditory problems. Single mum, doesn't know dad. Mum asked us not to send home any books about dads. Six months behind. No funding.

Abigail's birth dad is absent. Mum's new partner left the state with her money. She has an older sister who is highly anxious and scratches her face 'til sores appear. The children are aware of their stepdad stealing mum's money. Born premature, she has poor fine-motor skills and bone development and has difficulties drawing and writing. Abigail's school bag was full of rocks from the playground. She said she was collecting them to put in her house against the door so her stepdad couldn't get back in if he returned. She is repeating grade prep. No funding for OT (occupational therapist) support.

Chrissy has a spectrum disorder, a stutter, ADHD (not medicated), she is supersensitive to visual information and has a high oral fixation (chews everything). She has supportive parents, has been funded since kindergarten, has regular speech and OT, equine therapy organised by mum outside school and she is funded for two hours a day but shares aide with three other students.

Hope's parents separated in term one. Dad left and Hope is scared that mum will leave too. Hope is highly anxious at school drop-off times. She has low speech—difficult to understand, has trouble making friends as kids can't understand her. She sees a speech therapist fortnightly—but has no in-class support. She is twelve months behind academically.

Lucy has an oral fixation: she is constantly sucking her thumb or chewing on her school-dress collar until it is saturated. She has supportive parents who are both employed. She has poor fine-motor skills: her writing is unreadable and does not reflect what Lucy actually knows. Twelve months behind in writing, no OT support.

Arky's dad had a workplace accident, falling off a roof at a construction site the year before Arky started school, leaving him learning to walk again. The family was fully focused on

Dad's rehabilitation. Arky has no learning difficulties but no exposure to learning. He started school not knowing colour names or shapes, let alone ABC ... or 1, 2, 3 ... as most grade preps do.

Angel has supportive parents but she suffered with separation anxiety for the first half of the year. She is at appropriate level academically. Dad has own business.

Travis has supportive parents who are both employed. He is twelve months ahead in learning and plays several musical instruments at age five.

Hunter comes from a large family. Dad works in Melbourne. His learning is at the appropriate level. He has an older brother (year 3) with anger management issues who is medicated and was expelled from two schools before joining this school. Hunter is well adjusted.

Emma's parents both work, Emma is at [appropriate] level though her older sister has learning difficulties. Her parents are extremely supportive.

Mitchell was born premature and is small for his age, but he has no learning difficulties or physical challenges. Dad is employed. He is a happy boy.

No wonder I was burnt out.

I battled with my leadership for some sort of support—I even asked for one less yard duty a week—so I could catch up on emails from social workers, speech therapists to support the kids—but that was denied. I asked for a chance for the two aides who ended up job-sharing the class, for us to have a meeting once a fortnight. I was told this could happen but it was up to me to work out how. It was just too much for my graduate teacher brain to manage. I saw no other choice but to resign. I gave up my ongoing job, maternity leave, accumulating long-service leave and ten weeks of sick leave.

Emotionally—best decision I made. Financially— the toughest.

ANNA

Anna (not her real name) decided midway through our discussions that teaching had taken enough from her already and she didn't want to put any more time into it, go back to it or dwell further on what had become a traumatic period in her life. I suspect, too, revisiting her many experiences may have held little appeal but she also felt impelled to say something of how her contribution had been belittled, if only because saying nothing changes nothing. What I have reproduced here is only a part of her story, but I do value her insights and judgments (some of which she had previously shared on social media) coming as they do from more than thirty years in the classroom.

Why Australia is at the bottom of the educational outcome pile.

I don't really feel any enthusiasm for writing this as I'm just not keen on investing more of me in a system that burnt me out. It's taken enough already. I stepped out of teaching a year ago. I was completely over it. And I needed time away from it, away from the headspace of analysing it. To be honest, I'm not even sure I want to put any time into it at this point. I am now running a business, which keeps me very busy. I am very concerned for the future of Australian education but it may not be 'til I have grandchildren needing to go through the system that it comes to the forefront of my energies again.

A report on *60 Minutes* last night hit a raw nerve with me. As a flipping great teacher of thirty years' experience I have stepped out on stress leave this year and I truly don't know if I can ever go back. The absolute transforming joy of engaging students in the process of learning, of seeing them succeed when they thought they couldn't, or just loving something they thought they wouldn't, is priceless. It is why I worked twelve-hour days, every day, and worked half my weekends more often than not. But eventually I became broken by the system that was relentless in its need to add to my to-do list with administrative task after administrative task, change for the sake of change, and by parents who were empowered in the system to micromanage every aspect of their child's learning and throw blame at the drop of a hat in a teacher's direction.

So these are my thoughts on why Australia is now ranked 39 out of forty-one countries for educational outcomes in the developed world. The shift that has occurred in the Australian educational system that has seen our worldwide ranking drop to alarming levels and is causing quality, caring, dedicated teachers to leave the profession in record numbers is that the system has fundamentally morphed from a privileged right of a prosperous nation to a consumer-based product.

Teachers are no longer seen as a valuable resource in this quest for bettering our world through nurturing responsible, intelligent, creative young people. They are now simply seen as employees who just need to do what they are being told to do, by the educational academics, administrators and the parents. And the list of what they have to do to keep their job is increasingly being filled with administrative tasks to justify either their existence or that of the academics who keep coming up with them, leaving less and less scope for teachers to actually be the professional educators they were called and trained to be.

Why do teachers become teachers?

It is to change lives. It is to speak life and a love for learning into their students. It is to creatively engage students in the process of learning and leave them with the greatest gift for adulthood they could have ... curiosity, innovation and self-belief.

It is not to cross off a bunch of administrative tasks and pointless academic goals, to constantly be asked to prove themselves through standardised testing that robs all joy from the learning process, and to be PR machines, jumping when a parent says jump, pandering to a parent's need to micromanage their child's success.

To the school academics and the school administrators and the parents, I say, Back off! Respect your teachers and treat them with the professional regard they deserve, give them ownership for how they teach and they will reward you by putting their heart and soul into helping each child they are given to become the best learner they can be.

And if you really cannot trust teachers to do their job, then maybe look at the requirements to become one ... and introduce greater rigour at the front end so we get the brightest minds stepping up to teach ... but we have to make it enticing first ...

Dumbing down the entry-level requirements to get into teaching breeds less capable teachers which breeds further distrust in them which creates a more highly micromanaged system which causes the brightest minds to not even consider the profession because they want ownership of their processes. They demand the autonomy they know they can get in other professions.

So the brightest won't apply for teaching, so the entry levels go down further and so less capable teachers are bred, along with more distrust and more micromanaging, and fewer apply ...

It has to start now ... with the current generation of teachers ... Look after them well. Give them back their love for the job.

Make the intrinsic reward worth it.

Respect, honour, cherish and empower them.

Then maybe, just maybe, you might make it [teaching] something the brightest of this nation might yet aspire to do.

So stop the rot. Step back. Honour your teachers. Resource them well. Applaud them. And then look out, world, because Australia will be back on top of the educational outcome pile.

Personally, I am just really happy that I am out of it and my life is my own again. I don't have the quality of my life dictated to by navel-gazing academics who seem to have no clue. I am absolutely baffled as to how intelligent university-educated academics cannot see how monumentally they are stuffing up the system ... when there are successful models in countries like Finland showing exactly what we need to do to change things.

Unfortunately we have the culture here where we expect our governmental bodies to micromanage us, for fairness and our own safety. It just backfires terribly in situations like this where lack of autonomy is breeding a dull generation of teachers who are resigned to not being able to creatively impact the system ... generating better outcomes. The level of anxiety and social-emotional diagnosis of high-school students is now ridiculous—one more symptom of a system fundamentally flawed.

A MATTER OF PRINCIPAL

I meet with John over a couple of coffees at a local Italian restaurant. He arrives early and is keen to talk about the ideas of the Finnish education system my introductory email had mentioned. Fit and sharp, his grey hair is the only evidence of his years of teaching and sixty-plus years of age. As we speak, a picture emerges of a man dedicated to the profession and never afraid to be different, his loyalties often split between the needs of his teachers, students and the Education Department which paid his salary.

Like many teachers, he has a way with words. A few days after our first meeting he sends me an email telling me that our discussions have 'sparked my urge to do battle again, a battle which I generally say to friends I've given up years ago in order to maintain my sanity'.

You can take the teacher out of the school …

I came from a poor and non-academic family so the option of going to university in 1964 didn't exist for me. I had low motivation levels and didn't fancy working too hard at anything so staying at school and being paid for it seemed okay to me. Hence I applied for a primary teaching scholarship which would support me moneywise while I stayed at school. I got a scholarship on a second round of awards, thus I mustn't have been seen as a top candidate!

The only sound advice I ever got from my father was: 'Yeah. go into teaching. When you retire you will have a good superannuation fund [balance].'

I began teaching in 1966 with a two-year TPTC (Trained Primary Teachers Certificate) certificate and taught in a number of country schools until coming to Geelong in 1969 at South Geelong PS which, believe it or not, was seen as the roughest and least desirable school in Geelong: now it's very socially acceptable. In 1970 I was given twelve months' leave to teach in the UK which was like a rite of passage for many young Australians in those days.

When in England I taught at three very different schools each for one term. The first was a comfortable country town, the second a very poor industrial town, and lastly a comfortable rural school. At all three I was very impressed with the professionalism of the vast majority of staff. They were allowed to express their opinions and to implement their beliefs as long as they weren't strongly different to the principal's requirements.

The greatest impact on me was the nonexistence of a seniority system which was totally controlling, and stifling ideas and the advancement of education in Victorian government schools back home. At that time in the UK you had the principal at the top who could be quite independent of the system, then the deputy—who really was only a backup to the principal if he was absent, then all other staff were seen as equals except that the better teachers were given more respect by their peers, principal and the community. This was a big surprise to me and I think it influenced my teaching and administration beliefs for the rest of my career.

From a teaching point of view I saw three aspects practised which I had never seen or heard of before in Australia:

- Most classes allowed for, and taught to, different pupil needs—e.g. different groups for reading with different books with at least four to five groups, and mathematics broken into two or three groups, some working with concrete materials and some abstractly, and set assignments or projects which presumed that different results and standards were acceptable;
- The better teachers were using standardised tests to sort the pupils for their classroom management: I didn't even know what a standardised test was at that time. This testing was not used for parents or even other teachers' information: it was purely an internal matter for individual teachers;
- The use of experiential teaching, e.g. MAB blocks (multibase arithmetic blocks) for mathematics, cooking etc.

Upon returning to Australia I started using the aids and structures I had seen in the UK and, to be honest, they were extremely disliked and resisted by most teachers and even some principals. It's not until I move to the western suburbs of Melbourne in 1976 that I started to find teachers, consultants and the rare principal who believed in similar teaching methods—but still little support for lessening the teaching seniority system.

My more famous statements as a primary principal, which I made as far back as the eighties, were:

- At Tottenham in the early 1980s: 'Staff, you have my permission to do whatever you want for a term so long as the children develop the goals of wanting to come to school and to enjoy learning.' (If a principal said that now they'd be sacked!);
- Sunshine Heights in the late 1980s: 'Eighty percent of what we are teaching children today is a waste of time. Who knows what information or skills a ten-year-old today will need in twenty years' time to cope with employment and life?';
- Various schools and forums from the late eighties 'til I retired in 2000: 'Computers are just a tool, they are not real learning.' (I was viewed as a heretic for such opinions at that time.) Many of my concerns have turned out to be correct—i.e. the misuse of social media, loss of social and communication skills, the abdication of teacher responsibilities for all individuals etc.

In 1983 I became the principal of Tottenham Primary School via the old seniority system at the age of thirty-five as I was aggressively climbing the greasy pole, i.e. taking on positions most people avoided.

In the early eighties Tottenham and Braybrook were considered to be the toughest schools in Melbourne. When arriving at Tottenham I found a very rundown down school with poor discipline and attitudes. I arrive and within the second week, grade 6 kids literally belt the hell out of my female vice-principal, leaving her bruised and shocked. Staff threatened to go on strike ... I ousted the two kids immediately, told the parents: 'You've got thirty minutes to pick them up, we never want to see them again or I'm calling the police and having them charged with assault.'

Six months or so later the Director of Education, who'd obviously found out about this story, visits me one day and says, 'Do you know that you are not allowed to do that?'

I said, 'I don't care! It showed the parents and it showed the staff that they had a principal who was prepared to do something.'

But generally I could tell that the kids were just totally turned off, they didn't like school, they were feral, they were fighting, they had no respect for the teachers ... So I took this rash decision of saying, 'You have my permission to teach whatever you want, whatever you think they need to learn.'

Luckily, I had a very young staff who were willing to try new ideas as they had an attitude of 'We need to change but don't really know what we want to change to.' Hence my theories of top-down learning and experiential learning were taken on board quickly by some, which then spread to most staff by my second year. I am not saying all was plain sailing, but it helped that I supported the brightest and best teachers regardless of seniority or age.

Within three years Tottenham had become a pilot school for the system of 'creative writing' which characterised the features of top-down and open-ended learning. The region gave us strong support on the belief that if change like this could occur in such a disadvantaged school as Tottenham then it could occur in all schools. I should add that Tottenham was registered as a highly disadvantaged school, thus we did have a very generous staffing ration and ample money to buy equipment which did help my structures. This level of staffing and money for equipment has continually tightened and declined from the late eighties until today, and for the foreseeable future, I would guess. I feel that governments (of both colours) and Education Departments in the last twenty years prefer to spend new money on buildings rather than staffing and learning, for political reasons . I have taught in both disgraceful buildings and palaces, and the quality of the building has little impact on the levels of learning in my opinion, e.g. Tottenham was a disgrace; Clifton Springs was a palace.

Upon leaving Tottenham I was more removed from actual classroom learning as I was in bigger schools and was more involved in political matters across schools and regions. On reflection at the primary level I see schools or learning units with, say, 250 to 300 pupils with a teaching staff of fifteen or sixteen (this includes an administrator) better positioned to deliver real learning.

At the secondary level I am not an expert, but I am guessing that smaller schools and units than [are] presently existing would also do better.

In my mid to late 40s I had health problems that led me to giving up my principal's role. After sick leave I returned to teaching, but as a classroom teacher, for six years. This became a blessing in disguise as it allowed me to actually implement my beliefs myself for the first time in my career, as previously I had always been in an administrative role. Fortunately, I had a principal who allowed me to be as experimental as I wanted— providing I didn't try to be controversial in the staffroom or outside my classroom. I have some wonderful examples of personal successes with my beliefs, e.g. as such I didn't teach spelling all year, which my coordinator who taught a parallel class strongly disapproved. At the end of the year she wanted to give the same test to both classes which she did and even did it herself. She was shocked when my class performed better than her class overall!

Finally, as to why I retired: I still enjoyed my teaching, especially with my personal teaching, but I could see the writing on the wall—the impact of across-the-board standardised testing, the increasing demands of the department on schools combined with the reducing resources of a meaningful nature, and the lessening of respect for the profession across the wider community.

The final straw, although minor in truth, was the increasing insistence that I use computers to tabulate all of what the class and I were doing. 'Damn it,' I said. 'I am off!'

It is amazing how much I agree with all that I have heard about the system in Finland and the misuse of standardised testing by parents, politicians, press and society in general, uninformed teachers and certain education systems in this country. I have held my beliefs a very long time, which meant that I felt I was always swimming against the system and the majority of teachers, especially in conservative teaching areas like Geelong where I did much of my teaching.

I still believe in open-ended education (which resulted in some missteps in the eighties due to a lack of real understanding of the process) and in top-down learning[1] which I feel too many people have turned their backs on in the last twenty years.

---

1   A top-down teaching style focuses on providing students a large view of a subject, immersing them in the big picture without explaining the components that make up the subject. For example, in an English as a Second Language class, a top-down approach would begin by

Within the Victorian government system I am old enough to remember how we fought to introduce local selection of principals based on merit, which was later extended to include all teachers. I now think this has led to the discouragement of ideas and experimentation by progressive and thinking people in many schools for fear that to do so may hinder their careers.

---

immersing students in all aspects of learning English immediately, including writing, reading and pronunciation. Students would not be taught the intricacies of vowels, nouns and pronouns first, instead they would be plunged into the totality of learning English and then gradually learn the building blocks that make up the English language.

WHAT SHOULD THE GRADUATE SEEK IN A SCHOOL?

So you have completed your education studies and now want to start your teaching career.

Hopefully the stories from the teachers in the preceding pages will give some hints as to what to look for and what to avoid (also hopefully, they have not put you off teaching altogether!). I asked the contributing teachers (and principal) to provide exactly what information they believe a young teacher should be asking for in interviews (and before interviews) to avoid joining the estimated 50 percent of graduates who leave the profession within their first five years in the classroom. As a new teacher you may feel reluctant to ask questions, but the interviewing panel will be impressed that you have done some research and also will be gratified that you know something of what to expect as a career teacher.

If you find yourself in a particularly challenging school environment, the right principal will often be the difference between surviving or not. Alternatively, a good school situation can be made challenging by an inept principal.

Julianne gave excellent reasons for being careful when finding a job early in your career: 'It is okay to be picky about where you work even if you are a first-year graduate. It is harder to present your true happy self in a future interview if you are burnt out. Working in a happy environment is important for your mental health: you are no good to the kids if you are burnt out. Not everyone leaves one school because they are unhappy—but if you do end up in one school that is breaking you, you might not be strong enough to present well in an interview for a new school.

'So be picky from the start!'

'Ideally you want to apply for new schools when you are feeling at the top of your game, full of confidence and knowledge, and applying knowing that you will add value to your new school, not bringing baggage with you from a previous school.'

In addition to Julianne's advice about you being in the best shape when presenting for your next teacher interview, it's also worth considering that at the point of looking for your second teaching position the only key referee you may have is your first principal. Should there have been a less than ideal relationship here (as was the case with Julianne) you could find yourself trapped, not presenting well at interview and with the only referee being the person in part responsible for your troubles. This is where some emergency teaching work both before you commence your first position, and between positions later, can be a very convenient opportunity to gain further connections and learn about school environments. Movement within the government school systems in Australia is usually frequent and easy to do, but this is not the case in the private system where connections between other schools can be few.

As Dr Tomas Chamorro-Premuzic,[1] an international authority on psychological profiling, talent management, leadership development and people analytics, states—and I believe this applies to schools as much as it does business in general: 'Managers are the number one reason why people quit jobs. As the old saying goes, "People join companies, but quit their bosses."' (Chamorro-Premuzic, 2019)

Dr Chamorro-Premuzic also gives some advice on what one should be looking for in a leader. As a candidate, you will need to do some research to find the answers to these questions. However, this should be part of the research you would expect to be doing on the school and its methods before attending an interview for a teaching position.

Try to speak to as many people from the school community as possible. Teachers, former teachers, parents, students, and former students can all be of assistance.

---

1   Dr Tomas Chamorro-Premuzic is the chief talent scientist at Manpower Group, co-founder of Deeper Signals and Metaprofiling, and Professor of Business Psychology at both University College London and Columbia University. He has previously held academic positions at New York University and the London School of Economics, and lectured at Harvard Business School, Stanford Business School, London Business School, Johns Hopkins, IMD and INSEAD, as well as being the CEO at Hogan Assessment Systems. Dr Chamorro-Premuzic has published nine books and over 130 scientific papers, making him one of the most prolific social scientists of his generation.

1. *Is he or she (the principal) generally liked, or at least well regarded, by his or her direct reports?*

This would be consistent with the mainstream scientific view that upward feedback (feedback from those who work for the manager) is the best single measure of a manager's performance. If the answer is no, the probability that the principal is not the one for you increases dramatically. It is also worth remembering that when you apply for your next position, your previous principal is almost inevitably going to be asked to recommend you.

2. *Does he or she frequently provide staff with constructive and critical developmental feedback to improve their performance?*

Do they regularly talk with staff, in both formal and informal settings? Is there an effective performance review system in place?

Scott Mautz, the author of *Find The Fire: Ignite Your Inspiration and Make Work Exciting Again* and award-winning keynote speaker, put it this way in his advice to leaders: Give them the best feedback they've ever gotten.

It's not a high enough bar to merely invest the time it takes to give feedback. Any leader can do that, although clearly not every leader does. Research from Officevibe (an online leadership learning platform) shows that two thirds of employees want more feedback, and 83 percent say the feedback they get isn't helpful.

The best principals go beyond this and thoughtfully plan out and deliver insightful, actionable, even brave, feedback.

3. *Does he or she know their staff well and have an accurate picture of their potential, including their strengths and weaknesses?*

No principals can do their jobs well unless they are fully aware of what their team members can and can't do, which is a necessary precondition to assigning each employee tasks and roles where their skills and personality are best deployed. After all, talent is by and large personality in the right place. If you think your prospective principal doesn't want to know you, then he or she is less likely to be a good fit for you.

Scott Mautz again gave this advice to leaders and you should look for it in a principal:

Care about their careers as much as you care about yours.

Start by having crystallizing career conversations. Help them identify what they want to do in their teaching careers, not what they're *supposed to* want to do. Get clear with them on what it takes to get where they want to go, and discuss options without setting unrealistic expectations.

I found this in a number of the principals I encountered. They were wise enough to know that if I was to find success, then so too would the school and the wider education sector— and suggested Professional Development that they believed would be valuable to my further career even if it wasn't essential at my current school.

Education is not an adversarial profession.

4. *He or she seems truly coachable and continues to improve to the point of getting better on the job all the time.*

Just as your employability depends on your own ability (and willingness) to continue to develop key career skills and learn things that broaden your career potential, your boss should also be finding ways to get better. This means not just displaying the necessary humility and curiosity to learn—including from his or her own employees and customers— but also finding ways to keep their dark side or undesirable tendencies in check. In short, does the principal show self-awareness and the drive to get better, irrespective of whether that actually advances his or her own career? If the answer is no, then this principal may not be the one for you. (Chamorro-Premuzic, 2019)

Julianne recommends looking into relations between the principal and assistant principal. Where are their offices? Do they sit together, offices side by side? Do they appear as a united front or do you find them at opposite ends of the school?

Find out if the school has a high staff turnover. Teachers are reluctant to leave good schools and principals; high staff turnover is a sure sign of problems somewhere. Fábio D'Agostin suggests looking into questions such as 'Do teachers at your school enjoy their work? Are there examples of how professional enjoyment, satisfaction and fulfilment are achieved by staff in your school?'

Consider the same questions about students: *What makes students happy in your school?* Then, *what role would I play in becoming part of this happy, satisfying, fulfilling community?*

What does the school offer in extracurricular activities? Check the newsletter for evidence of these.

What is the specialist program like?

Does the school value art, PE, music, ICT (information and communications technology), STEM, sporting events?

What are the average class sizes? Are there many exceptions to this?

Does the school's 'values system' appear to match yours? I

know of one private school which sent a questionnaire to job applicants asking about their attitudes to homosexuality, sex before marriage etc.

Does the school have staff of different ages and experience? Julianne suggests, and I agree wholeheartedly, that you need mature, wise older teachers working alongside young teachers. Graduates need mentors and often a spokesperson.

Graduates supporting graduates is nice from a social perspective but shouldn't be the only support for new teachers in a school. Does the union have an active sub-branch at the school? Is the principal supportive of this[2] or does he or she see it as an enemy organisation trying to undermine the school? A school that is not supportive of the union presence may be involved in practices it wishes to hide from the union, such as exploiting the contract system, excessive class sizes and sub-optimal working conditions.

Julianne also points to the fair distribution of roles and higher responsibilities. 'Does the school have a merit and equity system and a number of staff trained in this? Government schools have had this in place for decades now, as has private industry. Do many of the staff apply for and participate in these

---

2   I am reminded here of one of my first principals, Br. Tony Smith, who attended all union meetings, and I saw him vote to go on strike, 'Anything that improves the wages and conditions of my staff is a good thing,' he announced before heading back to his office to put together a skeleton staff to cover those who were going out on strike. I have also seen other principals treat the union as an enemy to be excluded at all costs from the school's affairs. Finland has 95 percent membership of the teachers' union, and their professional standards and teacher qualifications are higher than nearly every other country in the world. Teacher wages there are similar to those in Australia. The union is there to assist teachers and everyone in the education system should be appreciative of this.

roles? A reluctance to take on these roles suggests that staff do not feel comfortable working with the school's administration for various reasons.'

Professional Development: Julianne continues, 'When people say, "Remember that maths game we learnt at that PD in 2017" and only two staff were at that PD because the rest have moved on and have been replaced … it makes it very challenging to build a consistent curriculum. Does the school encourage professional development? Is there a quota? Some schools like to see staff completing at least one day a term, and the principal or department head will follow up any teachers who are not doing so. A school that is not prepared to invest in its own staff will create problems for you further down the track.'

Look for information, and ask about parents, ratios, Indigenous students, special needs and the like. As you will find if you have read Julianne's story, administrative policy on all of these can be the cause of headaches for any teacher.

How does the school support students and families with extra needs?

Are there opportunities for students to show leadership? Do the student leaders have any real power or is it just tokenism?

Especially in a smaller school setting, what are the roles and responsibilities of the teachers? Is the team of teachers running the cross-country the same group of teachers running Book Week and choir? Is the distribution of roles fairly based on interests, and on the level of experience?

Rex Conner, in his book *What If Common Sense Was Common Practice in Business?*, talks about what he calls 'fuzzies', things that are open to interpretation or are completely subjective. He lists some of these:

- Your performance evaluation process;
- How promotion opportunities are evaluated;
- How your work is scheduled and assigned;
- How you are recognised for the work you do and the innovations you introduce.

Ask questions about these, not just in the interview but to anyone who may know the answers. When you drill down to the root of most workplace conflict, you will find the disagreement is over a work process that is subjective. Even a good boss will find it difficult to be good when they are trying to defend subjective work processes and systems. As W. Edwards Deming, the acknowledged Father of the Quality Movement, put it, 'A bad process will beat a good person every time.' (Conner, 2016)

The principal is usually the most important cog in your ongoing job satisfaction. Google employees are regularly surveyed about their managers with eleven specific questions. These fall into three general categories: nurturing growth in others, operating excellence, and emotional intelligence, all intended to discern the strength of a manager.

Here are some of the questions with 'principal' substituted for 'manager':

1. I would recommend my principal to others.

This is the ultimate test, no? It means as a leader and principal you must win employees' minds and hearts.

2. My principal assigns stretch opportunities to help me develop my career.

This requires you to care about your employees' careers as much as you do about your own. Find out what they aspire to (what they actually want, not just what they're supposed to want), discuss what realistically has to happen to get them there, and then leverage your network to help make things happen for them.

3. My principal communicates clear goals.

These goals should meet the three-Cs rule: common, compelling, cooperative. The commonality ensures everyone's working towards the same end. The goal must be compelling enough to create energy on its own and draw each person towards it. Finally, it should be cooperative in nature—lofty enough that the only way the goal can be accomplished is by the team working together.

4. My manager regularly gives me actionable feedback.

Ensure the feedback is specific and sincere (if it comes from the heart, it sticks in the mind). Keep a ratio of about five pieces of affirming feedback to one piece of corrective feedback. Nothing is more appreciated by employees than leaders who do this well.

5. My principal provides the autonomy I need to do my job (doesn't micromanage).

Manage by objective: give decision space and room for the empowered to operate without interference and oversight. Nothing is as powerful, productive and appreciated as being liberal with autonomy. It is one of the key traits of Finnish schools, yet one of the most difficult things for a principal to do.

6. My principal consistently shows consideration for me as a person.

People need to know you care before they care about what you know. The worst principals I ever had were always people who I could tell really didn't give a damn about me as a person. If your principal really cares about you as a person, everything else is likely to fall into place.

7.   My principal makes tough decisions effectively.

A close second on what burns out a school is an indecisive principal. Indecision is paralysing to a school. It creates doubt, uncertainty, lack of focus, even resentment. Multiple options can linger, sapping energy and killing a sense of completion. I was told of a principal who took more than an hour to decide if a teacher could go on a professional development training session (at the teacher's own cost), requiring release from about fifty minutes of teaching time. The decision was still not made at the completion of the hour.

8.   My principal shares relevant information from his or her boss(es).

Information should flow downhill, not be hoarded. Principals who withhold information to boost their own sense of control and power will soon be met with an organisation that feels out of control and powerless. If there is no transparency, what is being hidden?

9.   My principal has had a meaningful discussion with me about my career development in the past six months.

Think of how you'd feel if you knew you were working for someone who viewed themselves as your career champion. You'd run through walls for them.

Be aware that schools associated with any religion will usually find favour with those staff who are more closely involved with that religion. This can cause ill feeling among staff (particularly if they are from a background where merit and equity systems were in place) when leadership positions are not given to the most qualified candidates. A school where the best people for the leadership roles are not in those roles is not going to function effectively. Quality teaching staff may be ensuring that all looks well from the outside, but this will be far from the best the school can be. Staff who find their careers stalled are often stranded in these schools, their future path taken from them in a seemingly unjustified manner that can be soul-destroying for them.

All of the above will hopefully enable you to go into the interview prepared and give yourself the best chance of not just getting the position, but getting the position in the *right school* for you.

SUCCESS!

When you do obtain a position and have commenced your teaching career, remember the words of Dino Mangano, who wrote a book for just this reason: *New Teacher Survival Guide: How To Get Through Your First Year Of Teaching And Maintain Your Sanity.* Every teacher has days like the one Dino describes.

'You're driving home from work after a typical day at school and you're deciding if it's to be wine or beer. It's been one of those days that drain you completely. Not physically, but emotionally. Maybe that one student, the one who knows how to grab onto that last nerve of yours, said something especially mean and hurtful. Maybe your colleague down the hall who's supposed to be mentoring you has yet to give you any advice. Maybe your principal popped into your room to observe, and just stood there, writing on a clipboard without saying a word. Or maybe it was that most dreaded event, the negative parent phone call, with yet another parent wondering why you've been picking exclusively on their little angel.

'Whatever it was that has given you that crushed-soul feeling, you're starting to question if this is all worth it. Everyone seems so eager to take things out on you! What did you do to incur their wrath?

'The simple answer is: nothing. None of it has to do with you, none of it is because of you, and none of it is your fault …' (Mangano, 2019)

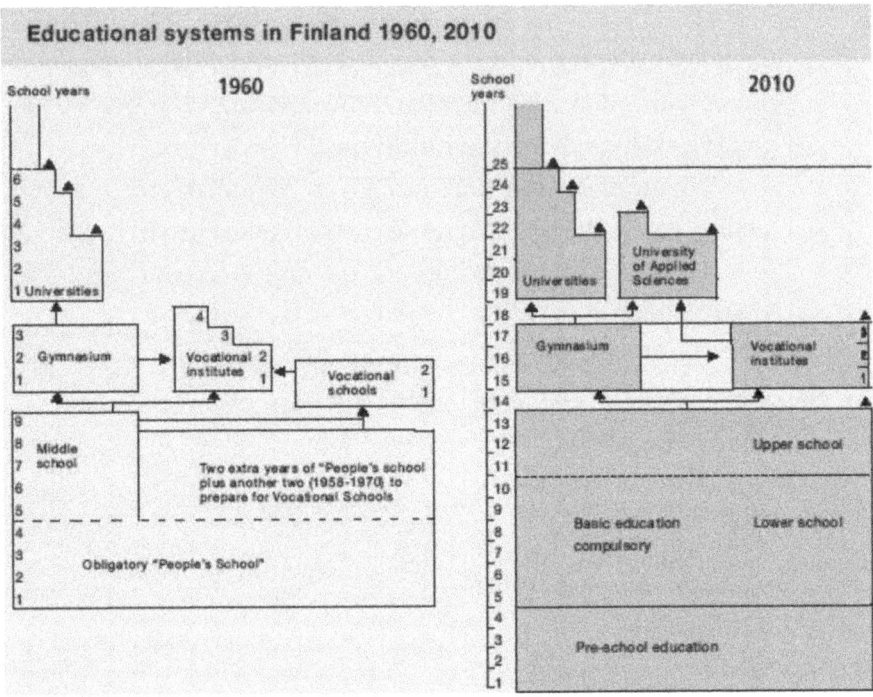

The old system (1922-1972) began with obligatory 'people's school' that everyone took. In the old days some people only took the obligatory four years due to issues like poverty. After four years, if you had 'head for education' or money, you went to the Middle school to prepare for the Gymnasium or took a couple of years more the People's school to prepare for vocational studies. Middle schools and gymnasiums were either private or public (called Lyceums) whereas People's schools were public. Very often people stopped their studies already at Middle school and went to work.

Basic education reform was done around 1972-1975. First nine years became obligatory and was the same for all. Schools are almost all public and main focus is to offer equal opportunities. From upper school students applied for either gymnasiums or vocational institutes and from thereon forwards to either to universities or universities of applied sciences.

There have been slight reforms but the basic system remains the same in 2019.

Bibliography

Aedo, C., Alasuutari, H., Välijärvi, J.: *Finland's 'education miracle' and the lessons we can learn*. (2017 5-July). From World Economic Forum: https://www.weforum.org/agenda/2017/07/finlands-education-miracle-and-the-lessons-we-can-learn

Alan Reid (2019 1-October). Gonski's vision of 'personalised learning' will stifle creativity and lead to a generation of automatons. *The Conversation*: https://theconversation.com/gonskis-vision-of-personalised-learning-will-stifle-creativity-and-lead-to-a-generation-of-automatons-124000

Aleksi Teivainen (2019 11-July). From *Helsinki Times*: http://www.helsinkitimes.fi/finland/finland-news/domestic/16557-studying-is-not-what-s-causing-mental-health-problems-says-student-health-expert.html

Amy Remeikis (2018 3-April). Educational inequality widening Australia's rich-poor gap, report finds. *The Guardian*: https://www.theguardian.com/australia-news/2018/apr/03/educational-inequality-widening-australias-rich-poor-gap-report-finds.

Anna Patty (2019 25-Feb). *The Age*. From theage.com.au: https://www.theage.com.au/national/nsw/down-to-individual-dot-points-school-curriculum-hampering-teacher-innovation-says-expert-20190225-p5101v.html

Aussie teachers working harder than their OS colleagues. (2018 Term 3). *Education Today*, http://www.educationtoday.com.au/news-detail/Aussie-teachers-working-harder-than-OS-colleagues-4178.

Berliner, David C. (2014). *Myths & Lies that Threaten America's Public Schools*. New York: Teachers College Press.

Bezos, J., e. b. (2018). *Jeff Bezos in His Own Words*. Chicago: B2 Books.

Blake Foden (2018 28-October). From *Canberra Times*: https://www.canberratimes.com.au/national/act/canberra-students-turn-to-sugar-daddies-to-pay-tuition-fees-rent-20181017-p50a48.html

Brett Mason, SBS News. (2018 31-January). *No school until age seven: Finland's education lessons for the future*. From SBSNEWS.com: https://www.sbs.com.au/news/no-school-until-age-seven-finland-s-education-lessons-for-the-future

Calla Wahlquist (2017 2-August). Naplan testing: students' skills show little improvements [sic] 10 years on. *The Guardian:* https://www.theguardian.com/australia-news/2017/aug/02/naplan-testing-students-skills-show-little-improvements-10-years-on.

Celina Ribeiro (2019 19-June). *A private school gets a castle-library, while we fundraise for public school music lessons.* From *The Guardian:* https://www.theguardian.com/education/commentisfree/2019/jun/19/a-private-school-gets-a-castle-library-while-we-fundraise-for-public-school-music-lessons

Chapman, G. & White, P. (2019). The *5 Languages of Appreciation in the Workplace and "Why Recognition Programs Don't Work" in The Vibrant Workplace.* Chicago: Moody Publishers.

Chris Bonnor and Bernie Shepherd (2017 21-June). We've been watching an unfolding disaster in schools for years. Gonski 2.0 could turn it around. *The Guardian* https://www.theguardian.com/commentisfree/2017/jun/21/weve-been-watching-an-unfolding-disaster-in-schools-for-years-gonski-20-could-turn-it-around.

Chung, J. (2008). *An Investigation of Reasons for Finland's Success in PISA.* Oxford: University of Oxford.

Conner, R. (2016). *What If Common Sense Was Common Practice in Business?* Charlestown: CreateSpace Independent Publishing Platform.

Couros, G. (2015). *The Innovator's Mindset.* San Diego: Dave Burgess Consulting Inc.

Darling-Hammond, L. (2010). *The Flat World and Education.* New York: Teachers College Press, Columbia University.

Darling-Hammond, L. & Bransford, J. et al., eds. (2005). *Preparing teachers for a changing world.* San Francisco, CA: Jossey-Bass.

David Aaro (2019 29-April). *Central Telegraph- 20-indian-students-die-by-suicide-after-failing-ex/3713754/.* From Central Telegraph: https://www.centraltelegraph.com.au/news/20-indian-students-die-by-suicide-after-failing-ex/3713754/

Davis, J. R. (2017). From Discipline to Dynamic Pedagogy: A Re-conceptualization of Classroom Management. *Berkeley Review of Education, 6(2),* 130-153.

Davis, J. R. (2017). *Classroom Management in Teacher Education Programs.* Cham, Switzerland: Palgrave Macmillan.

Dowling, T. (2019 30-May). *The Guardian.* From www.Theguardian.com : https://www.theguardian.com/lifeandstyle/shortcuts/2019/may/29/small-talk-finns-could-teach-us-art-of-staying-quiet

Duckworth, A. (2017). *Grit: Why passion and resilience are the secrets to success.* London: Penguin Random House UK.

Erkki Aho, K. P. (May 2006). Policy Development and Reform Principles of Basic and Secondary Education in Finland since 1968. *Education Working Paper Series No.2 (The World Bank)*, 1-155.

Eternity News. (2018 3-November). From *Eternity News*: https://www.eternitynews.com.au/australia/school-head-calls-gay-student-row-preposterous/

Evans, J. (2018 24-September). ABC NEWS. 'Naplan Stress led to Year 5 student's attempted suicide', principal says. Canberra, Australia.

Faulkner, P. & Simpson, T., e. b. (2017). *The Philosophy of Trust*. Oxford: Oxford University Press.

Friedman, T. (2005). *The World Is Flat: Moving from the Information Age to the Conceptual Age.* New York: Farrar, Straus and Giroux.

Gabrielle Stroud (2017 6-Feb). *Why do Teachers Leave?* From ABC News: https://mobile.abc.net.au/news/2017-02-04/why-do-teachers-leave/8234054?pfmredir=sm

Helsinki Times. (2018 13-March). From *Helsinki Times*: http://www.helsinkitimes.fi/themes/themes/education/15390-50-000-finns-support-initiative-for-free-upper-secondary-education.html

Henrietta Cook (2019 2-April). Principals sound the alarm on mental illness in primary school kids. *The Age*: https://www.theage.com.au/national/victoria/principals-sound-the-alarm-on-mental-illness-in-primary-school-kids-20190402-p51a25.html

Horvath, J. C. (2019). *Stop Talking, Start Influencing - 12 insights from brain science to make your message stick*. Dunedin: Exisle Publishing.

Johnson, S. (2016). *Wonderland*. New York: Riverhead.

Jorma Ollila (2019 7-April). Why Finland comes out on top on happiness and more. *Los Angeles Times*.

Joseph, B. (2018). *Why We Need NAPLAN*. Sydney: Centre for Independent Studies.

Julia E. Morris & Wesley Imms (2019 28-March). *Helping teachers 'practise what they teach' could help them stay teaching for longer*. From The Conversation: https://theconversation.com/helping-teachers-practise-what-they-teach-could-help-them-stay-teaching-for-longer-114078

Julie Szego (2019 18-March). *theage.com.au*. From theage.com: https://www.theage.com.au/national/victoria/teachers-are-copping-the-brunt-of-our-contemporary-ailments-20190314-p5145d.html

Lakshi De Vass Gunawardena (2019 19-July). *Finland's Education System Leads Globally*. From Inter Press Service News Agency: http://www.ipsnews.net/2019/07/finlands-education-system-leads-globally/

Larissa Romensky (2019 20-April). *Bullied and harassed teachers a significant problem in Australian schools, report finds.* From ABC Central Victoria: https://www.abc.net.au/news/2019-04-20/la-trobe-university-report-on-parent-and-pupil-bullying/11027080

Määttä, S. U. (15 July, 2013). Significant Trends in the Development of Finnish Teacher Education Programs (1860-2010). *Education Policy Analysis Archives,* Vol. 21 No. 59.

Malcolm Sutton (2019 20-May). *www.abc.net.au/news/2019-05-20.* From ABC News: https://www.abc.net.au/news/2019-05-20/bringing-arts-music-back-to-classrooms-after-20-year-decline/11124520?fbclid=IwAR0nFBFDMufg_XwyiWdJjaCQDhPQ_3yPjPjD63UEYXJuWTEeTrBCByAoiWz54&pfmredir=sm

Mangano, D. (2019). *New Teacher Survival Guide: How to get through your first year of teaching and maintain your sanity.* San Bernardino: Mangano Coaching.

Marc McGowan (2018 21-October). *afl.com.* From http://www.afl.com.au/news/2018-10-21/why-the-newage-coach-is-here-to-stay

Mariko Oi (2015 31-August). *Tackling the deadliest day for Japanese teenagers.* From BBC News .com: https://www.bbc.com/news/world-asia-34105044

Marzano, R. J. (2003). Classroom management that works. *Association for Supervision and Curriculum Development.*

McKew, M. (2014). *Class Act.* Melbourne: Melbourne University Press.

McKinsey and Company (2016). Where Machines Could Replace Humans - and where they can't (yet). *McKinsey Quarterly.*

Melissa Benn (2019 24-August). *The Guardian.* From *The Guardian (UK):* https://www.theguardian.com/news/2018/aug/24/the-only-way-to-end-the-class-divide-the-case-for-abolishing-private-schools

Menasche, D. (2013). *The Priority List.* Sydney: Allen & Unwin.

Michael McGowan (2018 6-July). *Private schools on funding hitlist actually increase their funding.* From The Guardian.com: https://www.theguardian.com/australia-news/2018/jul/06/private-schools-on-funding-hitlist-actually-increase-their-funding

Michael McGowan. (2018 11-Sept). From *The Guardian:* https://www.theguardian.com/australia-news/2018/sep/11/private-education-spending-in-australia-soars-ahead-of-other-countries

Natasha Robinson (2018 23-October). *NAPLAN analysis reveals where you live is more important than public vs. private debate.* From ABC NEWS: https://

www.abc.net.au/news/2018-10-23/naplan-analysis-reveals-state-education-report-card/10404316

Ollila, J. (2019 7-April). Why Finland comes out on top on happiness and more. *Los Angeles Times* .

Pallavi Singhal (2019 5-Feb). *The Age.* From theage.com.au: https://www.theage.com.au/education/naplan-out-of-control-teachers-say-test-eats-into-curriculum-20190130-p50ul5.html

Pasi Sahlberg (2018 1-January). From https://pasisahlberg.com: https://pasisahlberg.com/interview-teachers-need-a-sense-of-mission-empathy-and-leadership/

Pasi Sahlberg (2018 6-January). Too much control: Pasi Sahlberg on what Finland can teach Australian schools. *The Guardian,* https://www.theguardian.com/australia-news/2018/jan/07/pasi-sahlberg-finland-teach-australian-schools-education.

Peta Stapleton (2019 7-June). *Teachers are more depressed and anxious than the average Australian.* From *The Conversation*: https://theconversation.com/teachers-are-more-depressed-and-anxious-than-the-average-australian-117267

Peter Goss & Julie Sonnemann (2017 2-June). Gonski 2.0 is the best chance to end the funding wars. Then we can address other reforms. *The Guardian,* www.theguardian.com/commentisfree/2017/jun/02/gonski-20-is-the-best-chance-to-end-the-funding-wars-then-we-can-address-other-reforms.

Q & A (2018 8-October). From http://www.abc.net.au/tv/qanda/txt/s4892251.htm: http://www.abc.net.au/tv/qanda/txt/s4892251.htm

Ravitch, D. (2014). *Reign of Error.* New York: Vintage Books.

Richard Adams (2019 20-April). From *The Guardian*: https://www.theguardian.com/education/2019/apr/21/classroom-messaging-apps-expose-teachers-aggreession[sic]-parents

Richard Godwin (2019 31-May). *The Guardian.* From theguardian.com: https://va.news-republic.com/a/6697175756495127046?app_id=1239&gid=6697175756495127046&impr_id=6697461574078892293&language=en&region=au&user_id=6545015848582447114&c=sys

Ripley, A. (2013). *The Smartest Kids in the World.* New York: Simon & Schuster.

Robert Nelson (2018 29-November). Why it is (almost) impossible to teach creativity. *The Conversation,* https://theconversation.com/why-it-is-almost-impossible-to-teach-creativity-105659.

Robinson, K. (2015). *Creative Schools.* Great Britain: Penguin Random House.

Sahlberg, P. (2015). *Finnish Lessons 2.0.* New York: Teachers College

Press, Columbia University.

Sally Weale (2019 27-September). *Top of the class: Why Finland's schools are the envy of the world. The Guardian.* https://www.theguardian.com/education/2019/sep/27/top-class-finland-schools-envy-world-ofsted-education

Sarah Dingle (2019 21-February). *Teachers warn money isn't everything, as parties step up education pledges in election year.* From ABC.net: https://www.abc.net.au/news/2019-02-21/teachers-say-money-isnt-everything/10830004

Schwartz, T. (2011). *The Way We're Working Isn't Working: The Four Forgotten Needs That Energize Great Performanc* . New York: Free Press.

Scott Mautz (2019 19-June). *The Fulfillment Factory.* From www.inc.com: https://www.inc.com/author/scott-mautz

Sitomaniemi-san, J. (2015 20-November). Fabricating the Teacher As Researcher: A genealogy of academic teacher education in Finland. *Academic dissertation.* Oulu: University of Oulu.

Stroud, G. (2018). *Teacher.* Sydney: Allen & Unwin.

Sunday Herald Sun, (2019). *Private School Pain, Parents getting into debt to pay exorbitant education fees.* Melbourne.

TALIS - The OECD Teaching and Learning International Survey. (2019 4-July). From OECD.org: http://www.oecd.org/education/talis/

Tomas Chamorro-Premuzic (2019 21-March). *Business Insider*/News Republic.

Tony Moore (2019 4-March). *The Age.* From theage.com.au: https://www.theage.com.au/education/teachers-autonomy-vital-for-classroom-learning-inquiry-hears-20190304-p511pv.html

Uusimaki, D. L. (2013 24-March). *Teacher Education: Keeping up with The Finns? An interview with Dr Tuija Turunen.* From International Higher Education Teaching and Learning Association: https://www.hetl.org/keeping-up-with-the-finns/

Verkaik, R. (2018). *Posh Boys.* London: Oneworld Publications.

Wagner, T. (2014). *The Global Achievement Gap.* New York: Basic Books.

Walker, T. D. (2017). *Teach Like Finland.* New York & London: W.W.Norton & Company.

Webb, R. V. (2004). A comparative analysis of primary teacher professionalism in England and Finland. *Comparative Education,* 40(1), 83-107.

Weiner, L. (2006). Toward a conception of culturally responsive classroom management. *Journal of*

Teacher Education, 55(1), 25–38. doi:10.1177/0022487103259812 .

Weiner, L. (2003). Why is classroom management so vexing to urban teachers? *Theory Into Practice, 42(4), 305–312. .*

Wettrick, D. (2014). *Pure Genius.* San Diego: Dave Burgess Consulting.

Acknowledgments

Thanks to: Mikko Turunen—for all his diligent work in assisting me with connections in Finland and assistance while I was in his country. His enthusiasm for Australia, its music and its beer is unmatched by anyone from outside the country, and his knowledge and connections with Finland's education system are such that this book could not have been done without him—well, not with the Finnish perspective anyway.

Kimmo Hirvonen for his kindness and support during my Finland visits.

Deb Hodge who allowed me to put into practice some of the Finnish ideas which were quite different to the normal school routine here in Australia and sometimes were counter-intuitive to what she had been doing.

Bruce Connor, one of the few people I found in the Australian system who had been to Finland and understood exactly what it was about.

Dr Fábio D'Agostin, whose belief in the strengths of a system that actually considers the students' ideas, emotions and opinions to be important is as strong as my own. Your presence as a sounding board and co-contributor to the text has made this so much more than it would otherwise have been. I think the reason the NAPLAN test never included a question asking 'How do you feel about this activity?' is because nobody would have liked the answer.

Professor Ron Lewis, who has been a shining light throughout my educational career—from my first days at university to providing opinions on this work.

Julianne (not her real name), who relived the traumatising experiences of her first years of teaching and allowed me to share them in these pages. She is now the proud mother of a little boy, and has also been back in the classroom doing some emergency teaching. Not completely lost to the profession.

John Walsh; was on board immediately when he heard where I was going with this book and allowed me to share his story.

To my family and friends who have put up with my constant talk about education systems, my absences while researching (overseas or interstate) and my writing, meaning I was often mentally and/or physically elsewhere.

David Tenenbaum, publisher at Melbourne Books for supporting my instincts once again. And editors, Ken Haley and Ben Knight.

Many others have assisted along the way: Graeme Stewart, Jane Thompson, Tristan Phieler, Br. Tony Smith, Paul Lewis, Kristen, Bruce Muirhead, Gabbie Stroud, Bill Dickson, Matthew Yau, Trevor Bishop, Madeline Ottl, Mark Arkinstall, Mark Donohue, Ashley Latchford, Wayne Brewster, Miss Doolan, Simon Lewis, Christian Ryan, Graeme Duff, Theo D'Agostin, Jussi Hanska (thanks for the book too), Elina Syri, Saara Tahtela, Pia Loven, Kati Luhtarjarvi, Peer Meyer, Ralf Appelkamp and Nina Barnes (Silvia) for a German perspective.

The Author

Michael Lawrence is a schoolteacher whose classroom experience of more than 30 years, ranging from grade prep to year 12, spans music, English, history and other subjects in both government and non-government schools. While his previous book titles have been the definitive music biographies on Cold Chisel and Midnight Oil, his visits to Finland with its world-leading education system have led him to look closely into the Australian system within which he has spent his professional life – and question just why education across this vast land is in decline. He eagerly looks forward to the next few years bringing further visits to Finland, with time in schools and interacting with educators at all levels. For this latest book – part primer, part exposé – Michael read dozens of specialist books as well as dissertations on Finnish children's and teachers' education, in addition to a host of insightful interviews with teachers from Australia and Finland.

Michael lives near Geelong. When he's not trying to reform the Australian education system, he enjoys the Surf Coast. Weekends find him either catching fish or catching his favourite bands as often as possible. In general, he has better luck with bands.

Michael is keen to work with any school wishing to implement elements of the practical and proven pedagogies of Finland, Sir Ken Robinson and Pasi Sahlberg. He can be contacted at *micklawrence1@gmail.com*